For Jill,

with co~

(formerly ~~~~ of ~~~~
RMS)

Diamonds in the Darkness

GW00361821

'The Revd Dr Pat Nickson was one of the outstanding
Christian missionaries of her generation. The culmination
of her work was in establishing community-directed
health-care training in the war-torn Democratic Republic
of Congo. A lifelong member of the Church Mission
Society, Pat put her faith into practice at the highest international professional level. Whether at the World Health
Organisation or the Liverpool School of Tropical Medicine,
she always put the needs of the patient first. Using evidence
gathered from listening and recording at grass-roots level,
Pat applied her considerable scientific and teaching gifts to
develop and implement a lasting strategic programme. She
won the loyalty and love of colleagues and students alike.
Her love of Africa led her, as a Chester candidate, to being
ordained priest in Aru and to receiving her OBE not at
Buckingham Palace, but in the open air of Ituri. She
remains an inspiration and a model of true collaboration
between humanity and the Holy Spirit.'

(Bishop David Urquhart)

# Diamonds
# in the Darkness

## Revd Dr Pat Nickson, OBE

www.onwardsandupwards.org

Distributed by:

Upton St Mary's Parish Church, 'Holmleigh',
8 Church Road, Upton, Wirral, CH49 6JZ, England
Tel: 0151-677 1186
e-mail: office@stm-upton.org.uk
www.diamonds-in-the-darkness.co.uk

Copyright © Pat Nickson and the Editors, 2011

All rights reserved. No part of this publication may be reproduced or
transmitted in any form or by any means, electronic or mechanical,
including photocopying, recording or any information storage or
retrieval system, without prior permission from the publishers.

First published 2011

*British Library Cataloguing-in-Publication Data*
A catalogue record for this book is available from the British Library.

ISBN 978-1-907509-14-8

Designed and typeset by Caroline Waldron at
Kenneth Burnley Studios, Wirral, Cheshire.
Printed and bound in Great Britain

# Contents

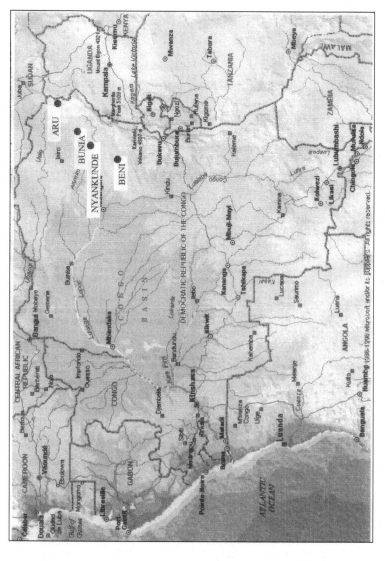

*Map of the Democratic Republic of Congo, showing relative positions of
Aru, Bunia, Nyankunde and Beni*

# Author's Preface

This book is one of memories, in which the Congolese community is seen by me as a foreigner, albeit with utmost appreciation of my Congolese friends and colleagues. These friends and
colleagues will see the text before it is presented for printing,
and will be able to change names and places where they feel
this is appropriate. There will be no identification of individuals
to whom this would cause embarrassment, while I hope that
identifying those who are the 'diamonds' would be acceptable.*

It is likely that other people interested or engaged in mission
in different situations will try to compare their experience and
expectations with mine. This book is about my memories and
cannot be compared with the memories of another person or situation, each of which has its own value and learning elements.

The history of the period covered by the book takes us through
name changes of the country as well as many other changes.
These are explained at appropriate places and changed as
necessary.

---

* *Use of names and stories – the editors have made every effort to fulfil Pat's
intentions. However, it has been difficult (or impossible) to contact and obtain
permission from all those whose names are mentioned.*

# Author's Introduction

In briefly introducing myself, the reader will walk with me through my professional training and experience into the much talked-about darkness of DR Congo. There we find exciting and thought-provoking stories of 'Diamonds in the Darkness' – people who have inspired and encouraged myself and others and who dismiss the stereotyped image of Congo as the heart of darkness. Rather, they reflect their faith and hope in God and how that can enable trust and love to be built and peace to reign even when there is pain and hardship. The stories will also take us into the lives of people of faith who have not been able to express peace and justice.

*Patricia J. Nickson*

# Editors' Comments

Pat's journey through life from July 1944 to April 2009 was an amazing adventure with God. Tragically losing both parents by the age of fifteen, her early academic achievements were not brilliant. But in 1969, after qualifying as a nurse/midwife and applying to the Church Mission Society (CMS) for missionary work, her life blossomed. God-given gifts of observing, listening, taking risks, vision, courage and intellect, coupled with a breadth of experience in Northern Australia, Afghanistan, Bangladesh, DR Congo, Côte d'Ivoire and many other parts of the world, equipped her to become an expert in the field of primary health care. She went on to train successfully many French-speaking Africans through the work of the Pan African Institute of Community Health (IPASC). In her late fifties, God clearly called her into ministry in the Church of England. Her last five years were spent on the clergy team of St Mary's, Upton, in Wirral, where her gifts of teaching and pastoral care were outstanding.

This book was started back in the 1990s and was intended to be an autobiography of Pat's life. She completed a fascinating chapter on Afghanistan, but work kept her from writing regularly. In 2007 Philippa Skinner, and later Ruth Daly, teamed up with her. From advice received, she set aside her early years and focused on DR Congo, where she spent the major part of her time from 1982 to 2004. Her dedication to serving others meant that the book still only occupied her spare time.

Chapters 1–3 were completed, Chapters 4–6 were mostly in note form. You will notice some duplication of stories in Chapters 4–6, where Pat has been slotting in extracts from different link letters but hasn't quite worked out where they fit in.

Chapters 7–9 were created when, in August 2007, she unexpectedly discovered she was terminally ill with cancer and had not too long to live – eighteen months as it happened. Pain and suffering became intense during the last few months of her life. With what energy she had, she devoted herself to others rather than the book. The limited words in Chapters 7–9 speak volumes, but sadly leave her intended book unfinished. The task of completing it is one that nobody can fulfil.

As far as possible, the content of this book is exactly as Pat left it. However, we have amended the fonts, layout and headings to distinguish the main (unfinished) narrative from the various notes and extracts from letters which she had assembled, presumably with a view to some more logical arrangement eventually.

So it may be best to see these later sections as you might view a collection of unthreaded beads . . . some might yet have been discarded, others trimmed for size or further polished; but all may be valued in themselves.

One of our team is still actively involved with both IPASC and the church in DR Congo. She has reminded us that it is the present and the future that matter, and it is our prayer that Pat Nickson's words will themselves encourage and inspire you as you read.

*Please visit the Diamonds in the Darkness website at http://www. diamonds-in-the-darkness.co.uk. You will find further background to Pat's life, many more photos, and inspirational stories of how Pat touched – and continues to touch – the lives of many across the world.*

# Acknowledgements

We are deeply grateful to the many people who have in some way contributed to the publishing of this book. However, a few individuals have spent much time and deserve a special mention by name. These include Revd Graeme Skinner, who downloaded much data from Pat's computer after she died, set up the Diamonds-in-the-Darkness website, designed the cover for this book, and took a number of the photographs included in the book. Also, Philippa Skinner and Ruth Daly spent hours with Pat encouraging and advising her in the earlier stages of the book (2007–8). Ken Burnley has been a tower of strength, encouraging us to publish and then taking on much of the work of copy-editing, typesetting and proof-reading, ably assisted by his daughter Caroline Waldron. Sue Simison helped us by meticulously proof-reading the final version. And Onwards and Upwards accepted the book and gave us the chance to publish. Last, but not least, a special thank-you to the IPASC family in DR Congo, the diamonds who inspired Pat to write and also brought such richness to her life.

*Gill Brown, Martin Daly, Jessie Hume,*
*Sally Shand, David Williams (Editors)*

# CHAPTER 1

# Steps on the Way to DR Congo

## Introduction

In the Akan culture, which I met in Côte d'Ivoire, the 'dja' is a small box or packet kept by each family, containing miniature representations of concepts, values and traditions of the culture. For example, a coffee bean might represent the importance of welcoming visitors. I was told that the 'dja' is opened annually by the parents, for the young people to learn about their ancient culture. With the 'dja' goes the mythical 'Sankofa' bird that flies forward while looking back over her tail, and with an egg in her mouth, the egg symbolising the future. The significance of this is that before making decisions about change, we should look back to our 'dja' and compare new ways with old and only then make changes if the new is better than the old.

This chapter brings together the contents of my 'dja', the concepts, values and different cultural traditions upon which my life in Congo was built. As I went into a new culture and a completely new life, these were the things I looked back on, and which I cherished. They equipped me with my 'dja' which taught me how to live and work in other cultures, and in my own culture.

## Early days (1944–62)

As the fourth of five children, in a loving home, family life was special but came to a premature end with the death of my father when I was eleven. To help my mother, I was sent to the Royal Masonic School in Rickmansworth, Hertfordshire, with my younger sister, Nikki. It was a very happy experience for me, though it was during my time there that my mother died.

Never having excelled at school, I had no hope of a career based on a university education, so I followed nursing, midwifery and health-visitor training. As a Christian, I had a deep interest in mission, which was heavily influenced by Harry and Ethel Parsons, foster parents who had been missionaries with the Church Mission Society in Nigeria. Harry was the vicar of my home parish in Polegate, Sussex. I applied to CMS before gaining experience in Australia.

## Training with CMS (1970–71)

CMS required me to do a year's training at Crowther Hall, one of the Selly Oak group of colleges for mission training. It was hard to settle into the academic part of training, but I revelled in the practical activities such as learning how to substitute a fan-belt with a pair of tights (this may have been useful for Afghanistan, but hardly in tropical countries!), and learning about other cultures from ethnic minority families in Birmingham. Each student was attached to a family, who had come from a culture similar to that to which we were expecting to go. I had been located to Afghanistan to work in a rural health programme, and so was linked to a Pakistani family in Birmingham.

The Ramazan family taught me much about family life in Pakistan, and allowed me to share their life in Birmingham. They invited me to many of the Muslim feasts and festivals and to family celebrations, and they came to Crowther Hall on several occasions, for parties, or just for fun with the college children. When Begum was in hospital with complications during her pregnancy, I baby-sat when necessary. Mr Ramazan wanted to know all about the complications that his wife was experiencing. His concern for Begum was touching, and we often visited her together.

Fatima, the eldest daughter, had always wanted to be a nurse, and had applied to the local hospital for training. On the day of her interview, she asked me to join her mother to talk with the Matron. During the interview there was a discussion about the uniform. At that time, student nurses wore dresses but Fatima's culture demanded that she cover her legs. The Matron could not make exceptions, although many of her patients would have been from a similar culture. So, although Fatima had passed the entrance exam, she had not passed the cultural test, and was not admitted.

I was learning that mission life was more about friendship, learning and receiving from others, than about teaching and giving. My friendship with the Ramazans taught me so much that, when CMS located me to Afghanistan, I had confidence to make friends both in Kabul and in the mountain villages.

## A missionary or just a good friend?
## (Northern Australia 1969–70)

Having spent years in various types of training, I was a well-disciplined nurse/midwife by 1969 when I went to Angurugu and Oenpelli, mission stations in the Northern Territory of Australia. But there I found that my 'correctness' got in my way. Let me give you an example. In my early days at the small hospital at Angurugu, on Groote Eylandt, Mike and Peter, Aboriginal brothers, were looking for fruit in a tree. Six-year-old Mike was in the tree with a small axe to cut the fruit, while Peter stood below to catch the pickings. Unfortunately, while cutting, the axe slipped from Mike's hand and fell on Peter's head. He was rushed to the nearby hospital where I was working in the pharmacy. Immediately I attended to Peter as I would have done in any hospital in Melbourne or London. I dealt with his fairly severe head wound, and then put him to bed in a darkened room, with only his mother beside him. I monitored him every fifteen minutes and would not let anyone visit him, although he was conscious and seemed to be doing well. A little later, I heard wailing coming from the lower end of the village. I asked my colleagues what was happening, only to be told that Peter's grandfather was dying. I was surprised because he was the one who carried Peter into the hospital. I gathered together some emergency equipment and ran in the direction of the wailing.

The old man had collapsed, and clinical observations showed that he was in a bad way. But why? I could find no reason, nor could the family give a history that would make him at risk from such a sudden collapse. All the family could say was that 'he will die before Peter'. 'Before Peter,' I remarked. 'Peter's not dying.'

'He must be,' the family answered. 'You won't let us see him, and he is in a dark room like the dying people.'

Grandfather Lalara was admitted to the same room as Peter, the blinds were drawn back, and visitors allowed in. I went off to catch up on sleep. A few hours later I returned to find the ward empty. 'Where are Peter and his grandfather?' I asked. 'Look!' I followed my colleague's pointing finger. There, among a crocodile of schoolchildren, was Peter with his head bandaged, but frolicking around like the rest of the children. 'And his grandfather?' 'Oh, he took a little while longer to get better, but now he's gone home. You see, sister, in our culture, the grandfather must die before his children, let alone his grandchildren.' I stopped trying to get the pharmacy straight and spent days in the bush learning more about the culture of the Anindilyakwa people. I had learned an important lesson.

My second post in North Australia was at Oenpelli. It was a beautiful spot with spectacular escarpments, mangrove wetlands and plant and animal life. Among my friends were those who were skilled at making bark paintings, some of which I still treasure today. It was easy to get to know the Gunwingu people and some of their culture because I was 'adopted' into the family of one of my colleagues.

One of my responsibilities was maternity care in the community. There was very little early ante-natal care given, and complications of pregnancy were frequently seen and made me determined to improve the situation, but I went about this in a clumsy way. Frequently, when I suspected that one of the women was in early pregnancy, she denied it. One day, when I asked a friend if she was pregnant, she said that she wasn't because her husband had not had a 'rainbow dream'. Apparently, in that culture conception is said to occur after a spirit child appears to a man in a dream. In that dream, often associated with another spirit, the rainbow snake, the spirit-child will ask to be born, and may ask where his mother is. As I became more familiar with this important cultural expectation, I noticed that the dream seemed to happen when, in biological terms, the mother was around five months pregnant, but it could also occur months before any biological conception. So ended any attempts at early ante-natal clinics. Instead everyone had 'ante-natal care': mums, dads and children. All were checked for anaemia and intestinal worms, and I managed to check most women's abdomens, but no one complained.

Had I stayed longer, I am sure that we could have built on these important lessons in culture which grew out of the generous friendship that the Aboriginals shared with me. To other missionaries I was seen as 'young and vulnerable' because of my frequent visits into the villages and walks along sacred routes with Aboriginal friends. I learned about the sacred bones among the rocks, the stories of the large clusters of rock and of the billabong. These experiences left me asking myself whether I should be a 'missionary' or just a good friend . . . In my early days in North Australia, I found that few people, and especially children, came near me. However, once I started making friends I could visit homes and share in family life. Then there were children all around me. Most of all, I learned how important it was to listen to local people.

## Afghanistan – rich in beauty and in culture (1971–74)

Afghanistan was completely different from North Australia, and yet the lessons I learned in Angurugu and Oenpelli were important. Listening to the culture through friendships was not difficult in a country with a rich culture and the incredibly friendly community in the central mountainous area of the Hazarajat.

In the winter, the Yakaolang Valley, where the Medical Assistance Programme (MAP), of which I was a member, was situated, was like a winter wonderland. Our house in the village of Nayak commanded the most superb view of the valley where everything was white except the clear blue skies. Temperatures were extremely low at night until the bright daytime sun broke the painful cold. It must be one of the most beautiful spots on earth, but it would take an artist to describe the beauty, magnificence and peace of the Yakaolang Valley.

From the sleepy days of winter the valley awoke to the full glory of spring towards the end of March. Very quickly the whole valley became dressed in a lovely green, with tiny bright flowers dotted over the mountain slopes. Brilliantly coloured birds took up residence in the willow trees by the river, and the cuckoo sang from morning till night. Pairs of oxen began ploughing, while boys and girls made their way down to the river, whistling as they carried their heavy water-pots on their heads or shoulders.

When riding my horse down the valley, I was often invited into homes and given naan (local bread) and green tea, while Foxy (Foxbury), my horse, was taken and fed. Morium, a girl about eight years old, had a habit of coming to our house, with or without her cow in tow, to take me to visit yet another family. Some village friends made me a Hazara costume. It was colourful and attractive, comprising a mid-calf-length dress, and very full pantaloons in a contrasting colour, with tight ankle bands. A colourful waistcoat fitted over the dress, and was ornamented with coins and other medallions. The head-dress was a bright red piece of material that reached the ground. I wore my new outfit to family celebrations such as at Eide Fityre (the end of the Ramadan fast) which were very lively and were always accompanied by superb food, served on dishes placed on a cloth on the floor. On some special occasions the villagers played Buzkashi, the national sport. Played on horseback, Buzkashi has few rules – certainly no apparent rules of 'foul play'. The objective of the game was for the riders to grab the carcass of a beheaded goat from the ground while galloping and then get it into a central goal. Competition is fierce and brutal. National players train for many years, as do their horses.

Women in the Hazarajat had never had a choice of where to go for childbirth and depended on the mother-in-law to be the midwife. Women frequently died in childbirth, and so anything we could do to reduce the mortality rate became a priority. Often at Nayak I was called out at night and would ride through the dark, always accompanied by a male member of the patient's household. I had special waterproof saddlebags made for Foxy – one to carry the small anaesthetic machine and another my obstetric instruments. Foxy swam through rivers easily and was sure-footed along the mountain tracks. In the homes I would be given every courtesy and consideration; but responding to a difficult situation for the mother or child, in poor lamp light, or, more often candle-light, while squatting on the floor, was not easy. Often I was professionally way out of my depth, but God's grace was given in abundance at those times.

Once the necessary intervention had been completed and the mother was comfortable, and Granny was nursing the tightly swaddled infant, I would be 'put to bed' – tucked up on a comfortable mattress, placed over the underground fire. Strangely, it was always the male hosts who 'put me to bed', but then, the many metres of materials in my clothes were not very revealing. I was nicknamed 'madar-e-kalon' ('the mother of all children' or 'Grandmother') – seemingly an insult but said as a compliment.

The whole of the community health programme was tremendously rewarding. I had particular fun teaching our first woman worker, Khatijah, who rode on Foxy behind me as we went together to the villages dotted along the valley. Training an illiterate health worker was a new experience for me, and for a woman to be allowed to go so far out of her village without male accompaniment was a novelty for her. But, somehow, it reflected the trust we were gaining, and taught me more about the culture and how health care needed to be moulded around cultural norms and expectations.

Often, on days off, I would stay in the village of Gumbazi with Khatijah and her family. During the day the women would sit together weaving large rugs, using wool from their sheep. The children would be playing around using home-made balls or dolls made from mud. In the evening we sat round the fire enjoying the relaxed atmosphere. Bedtime came quickly when it was dark (lamps were too expensive to use when they were not necessary). In the women's bedroom, the wives would ask me about myself, my family, my work and my faith. They too shared similar details with me. They were warm, open and generous, and were anxious to learn about the outside world. Putting all aspects of life in Yakaolang and in the village together, I counted it a privilege to have lived among such a community. Parts of the Hazara and Afghan culture and faith will always live with me.

## Bangladesh (1975–79)

When I arrived at Bollobhpur, two miles from the western border with India, I had an unbelievable welcome, with singing and garlands placed round my neck! My home was a beautiful old house shared with three other English women. Sitting on the verandah and looking beyond the lawn and the palm trees there was a quietly flowing river, with lilies and reeds resting near the banks. Colourful birds darted in and out of the trees, and the river farmers were irrigating their fields, using hollowed-out logs to scoop water from the river into the fields. Bright red flame trees, bougainvillaea, and other colourful shrubs and trees framed my picture. The happy voices of children were coupled with the distant shouts of the fishermen, and the brain fever birds competed in earnest. This was Bollobhpur – my first impression was that it was a place of beauty and peace!

On the other side of the house, however, there was bustling activity. Bethany hostel, with 80 grubby but delightful school-children, was just beyond the hospital gates. It was run by the Church of Bangladesh, as was the hospital which was beside our house, and which had 35 beds with patients suffering a wide variety of complaints.

As in much of Bangladesh, there were paddy fields all around us and so the diet included brown rice, rice pudding, puffed rice, rice porridge, rice cakes, rice milk and boiled rice! Sometimes we were able to get bananas and had an abundant supply of tomatoes. When the rains failed or were inadequate, people began to worry about the rice and jute crops. Failure of rains led to an exaggeration of the existing poverty and an increase in health problems. On the other hand, too much rain could do a lot of damage. Two years running, Nityandapur health centre was wrecked.

There were few roads or tracks in the area, but in the dry season we could reach most places by Land Rover. Crossing the wide river with the Land Rover was always a challenge. The ferry comprised bamboo poles strapped together to form a platform which was balanced across two small boats. Driving onto the platform at the wrong angle could overbalance the ferry, tipping the Land Rover into the river! During the rainy season we used our small boat, which had an outboard motor, to get to the villages or health centres. As we went down the river in our boat, we passed fishermen paddling or punting their little boats, while on the banks were mud huts with thatched roofs, nestled among palm trees and tropical shrubs. Occasionally a boy ran along the bank, carrying a banana leaf to shelter him from the driving rain. Reaching the health centres away from the river was more difficult as we needed to use a bullock cart – a bumpy means of transport moving at an average of three miles an hour.

Daily activities were punctuated by the presence of two small girls, Shondha (the moon), who was several months old when I joined the staff at Bollobhpur, and Tara (a star), who joined us when she was about two years old. They were cared for in Bethany Hostel, next door to the hospital.[1] Often the girls would come over to play in our garden and would accompany me when I was going out to some of the health centres. As soon as the car (or bullock cart) left the hospital grounds, the girls began to sing in the delightful Bengali way, and continued until we reached our destination!

Many people have described the area as one of the most difficult in which to work because of the hot and humid climate, the extreme poverty and coping with the violence and corruption. All that was true, but there were also some very positive things about Bangladesh, and especially Bollobhpur, that I learned during my five years there.

## Monika

Monika was a star. She had qualified as an assistant nurse, but had exceptional leadership and teaching skills and loved being in the community. In her early twenties, and married with two children, her determination, pride in her work and energy, earned her the respect of the village. Together we surveyed the health of communities around Bollobhpur and around the five sub-centres (health centres) which gave a total population of 40,000. We trained village health workers using the manual a couple of us had written in Afghanistan, purchased a village house and made it into a nutrition rehabilitation centre, managed the primary health-care work of the hospital and health centres, and established an extensive programme of community health. Monika had an insatiable appetite for developing new ideas and yet did not go beyond her own capacity to supervise the wide range of community health activities.

In the hospital, some of the senior staff had a similar capacity, but had never been allowed to climb above the role of 'staff nurse'. This meant that the (foreign) Nursing Sisters coped with much more than necessary. Monika, however, became head of the community health programme, because she was clearly more able than I was to handle the large programme which was now attracting visitors to come and learn from us.

Occasionally we would spend a day out, just sharing together and relaxing. I learned that life at home was anything but easy for Monika. Her ability and reputation did not help the situation, as she was stepping way beyond the normal role of a village woman, and yet her passion for her work and the encouragement she had to develop ideas, spurred her on. On those days spent relaxing with Monika, I learned a great deal about the upbringing of children, the respective role of women and men in the household, cultural patterns and expectations, and educational constraints.

Despite Monika's commitment she occasionally failed to arrive for work and I learned that this was when she was beaten by her schoolteacher husband for no explicable reason. When the situation became serious it was her husband who was admitted to hospital feeling sorry for himself, and was treated for depression. Mother-in-law and a younger brother were also involved in the domestic problems. Sadly, similar situations occurred in other educated Christian families in which the wife was working.

The Bollobhpur community health programme grew, and attracted visitors because of its innovative developments. Frequently Monika and I attended meetings of the Christian Health Care Project, an ecumenical umbrella programme, and Monika was asked to help with other programmes. Eventually her reputation won the attention of the Government and, despite her lack of higher qualifications, she was invited to teach at nursing schools and on health visitor courses.

To give space for the village health workers to learn more about their faith and to express themselves, Monika suggested that we start a Bible Study group. This immediately became popular and it was exciting to see how the lessons learned in discipleship and times of discussions changed their attitudes and behaviour. Most of them were third- or fourth-generation Christians and had never discussed their faith outside church and the daily chapel service. What seemed to be more important was giving space for like-minded women to be able to share their common joys and problems together.

**An old man on his way to heaven**

Our old carpenter taught me an important lesson. He had become very weak, but was still able to get around. One day he sent a message down to the hospital to tell me that he wanted to see me, because he was dying. I was busy with the ward round, and had only visited him the day before so did not understand the urgency of the request. Towards the end of the morning, I went to his house in the village. The little pathway to the mud and thatch cottage was full of people – mainly family. The old man was lying on a make-shift bed among the crowd. I sat with him for a short time as he slowly articulated his thoughts. Then he surprised me by saying, 'I am going now, Sister . . . Look after my daughters . . .'

From a medical point of view, his condition was probably reversible, but he was ready to go. As we prayed, he stretched out his hands and blessed his daughters. How very reminiscent it was of the Old Testament, and we could also add 'and he was gathered to his father's kin'. For me, this was a very moving experience as I joined with the family to share those last moments. It was a new experience because I am usually called to cure someone, not to sit with them as they die. And I learned something from the peace of that moment when an old man, convinced of his own salvation, absolved from the sins of his earthly life, had the courage to say quite calmly, 'I am going . . .', and to say it with such conviction that he just let go and fell into the arms of his Master.

## Jamaica (1981)

On a study trip to Jamaica I found an island of contrasts. To the tourist it presents palm tree beaches, sand and 'reggae music', while to the peasant it is home, hard work with meagre remuneration and a complicated family life. The visitor may be impressed by modern buildings and a sophisticated way of life, while the public health inspector complains of poor water supplies, insanitary housing and overcrowding. There is a wide chasm between the rich and educated, and the poor and unemployed.

The people of Jamaica are diverse, coming from African, Asian, European and Chinese ethnic backgrounds; descendants of slaves and rich plantation owners; of explorers and native Indians. Their culture is subtle, but also colourful and gregarious, with music as the nation's heartbeat, and religion as its soul, together pervading every aspect of life.

A country in the transition stage of development, with a colonial history, Jamaica has fine institutions but its development is handicapped by severe financial and trained human resource shortages. A tiered system of health care offers primary health care at community and health centre levels, with secondary and tertiary care readily available.

Family life in Jamaica is unstable, but has always been and so is accepted as the 'norm'. The fact that teenage motherhood and the influences exerted on the young mother was the focal point of my study should not suggest that it is a new problem, or even that it is necessarily a problem at all. It is an aspect of life which demonstrates how a 'comprehensive health programme' may not be comprehensive enough. Health care in Jamaica follows Western patterns, and so is not necessarily appropriate to the situation. For example, the teenage mothers were given health education and were encouraged to come to clinic with their children. Yet the child's grandmother or great-grandmother, giving the major part of the care to the child, could often be seen giving the infant 'marijuana tea' (an infusion of cannabis)[2] in a bottle, traditional medicine for coughs and colds, and various different forms of time-honoured, rather than contemporary, care.

The experience of studying in Jamaica helped me see how, in developing countries, health services are often modelled according to international norms and expectations rather than responding to the hazards and resources in the community.

## Conclusion

So what are the concepts, values and different cultural traditions that I have collected in my 'dja' before stepping out into a life in Africa? What will the Sankofa look back on from my life in other cultures, as well as my own culture? What changes will she allow and what experiences will she maintain as building blocks for the future?

My close family life, albeit short, and my involvement with families in various situations, affirmed for me the importance of family unity and its heavy dependence on the mother. Yet, in so many circumstances, the girl-child's educational and social needs are neglected and the mother's health and well-being often not considered.

Listening to people and making friends was an important part of understanding mission. Such friendships introduced me to new cultures and customs; and taught me that the local way of doing things was often the best way, given the respective context. Similarly, working with illiterate colleagues brought me to the heart of the community, where I could learn about health, healing, death, development and the social structure of the community. It also allowed the community to get to know me, and understand a little of my cultural heritage.

With these special values in the 'dja', the Sankofa can fly ahead and hatch her egg.

*The five: Gordon, Francis, Marian (Nikki),
Elizabeth and Pat, 1951*

*Pat in Australia, 1970*

*Pat with Shondha and Tara, Bangladesh, 1978*

# CHAPTER 2

# Setting the Scene in DR Congo

## Called to Zaïre

In 1980, while on study leave from Bangladesh, the Church Mission Society (CMS) asked me to be part of a group looking at a recent feasibility study of a health and development programme for what was then Zaïre (to become the Democratic Republic of Congo [DR Congo] in 1997). From a professional point of view I was interested in the study and the potential programme. Then I experienced one of those moments when one feels both drained and enriched, when the Holy Spirit is a silent but an overwhelming presence. Was the Holy Spirit directing me away from Bangladesh to Zaïre? Certainly the study I was doing at the Liverpool School of Tropical Medicine would be preparing me for such a move.

Zaïre, a former Belgian Colony, is a largely Christian country. In 1896, Apolo Kivebulaya, a Ugandan Anglican missionary, went to Boga, situated on the hills rising to the west of the River Semliki which forms the border between DR Congo and Uganda. With some 80 young men and women 'disciples', Apolo established a Christian community which reached westwards to the pygmies of the Ituri Forest. Before his death in 1933, there were over 50 small chapels and more than 1,500 baptised Christians. The work of the Anglican church has since spread across the country, which is the size of Western Europe.

## Life in Boga

Eighteen months after that 'call' to Zaïre, in February 1982, I was sitting in the *rondaval* – a small round hut which was my first home when I arrived at Boga, listening to the African harmonies coming from the cathedral nearby.

Set on the western escarpment of the Rift Valley, Boga has a magnificent view of the River Semliki and across to the Rwenzori Mountains in Uganda. The cathedral and 'mission' area of the village are peaceful, the only sounds being from cows, chickens and crickets. Typical of rifts, tectonic activities in the area result in frequent earth tremors, with the sound and vibration of approaching and retreating underground trains. The rift also exposes many minerals, making the country rich, though the minerals are pilfered for personal gain (of locals and foreigners) rather than mined for the benefit of the country.

I quickly adapted to the very basic life at Boga. One of my first trips out took me into the forest area where the pygmies lived. The forest was beautiful. It was like walking non-stop through a cathedral of trees, with attractive small butterflies hovering over pools of water. At a clinic in the forest, I examined a young girl, who I thought had a very large ovarian cyst. Then the 'cyst' kicked me. I was so glad that I had no Swahili – so had not got as far as telling the pygmy that she needed surgery. All she needed was a safe delivery. Apparently she was the mother of three healthy children and pregnant with her fourth. I had thought she was a child, not realising how small pygmies were. I certainly had a lot to learn!

Boga Cathedral, a very simple building, was the centre of the village and the mother church of the diocese. It was simply furnished, with the pulpit, font and table cut from trees planted by Apolo. For festivals and celebrations it was decorated with banana leaves and palm leaves, as well as colourful flowers.

Mission partners and senior church staff lived near the simple but attractive cathedral and hospital compound, which had moon-flowers, golden glory and bougainvillaeas and some tropical fruits (mangoes, avocado, paw-paw and guava).

Amoti Kabarole,[3] a 58-year-old widow and mother of seven children, was one of the key people on the community health team. Her husband was one of the disciples of Apolo, and was the first Zairean to be ordained. Amoti was untrained, but very experienced. She was competent, committed and tireless, and her wisdom in decision-making was dependable. Amoti went out on almost every health safari, each of which lasted two to four days.

She was responsible for weighing babies and advising mothers on child care. Often she recognised the distressed mother trying to hide the real cause of her child's malnutrition and, by tactful encouragement, established the reason for the distress – the husband was ill and could not work, or the mother had no husband and was dependent on prostitution to get money, though not enough to feed her children.

When I joined the team in 1982 there were two health centres, and eight health clinics which were held in schools or churches. Twenty to thirty patients were seen at each clinic, and up to 100 children were weighed and vaccinated. Pregnant women were given their regular checks and advised to stay in a village with a health centre when the time came for delivery. In those early days, some of the men would come when they saw that there were only a few women remaining. They were usually those with TB, leprosy or other chronic diseases, who found it difficult to walk to the nearest health centre.

On the safaris we would stay overnight with the family of the vicar or church leader.[4] Often, in the evening, I would sit on a mat with Amoti pounding peanuts and trying to improve my Swahili. We shared a meal with the family and learned more of life in those very rural areas. Amoti taught me some of the traditional ways of bringing up children, and what the normal expectations of a daughter-in-law were in her husband's family. The young mother had plenty of support, provided she conformed to the family's standards. However, with too much initiative and will-power she could find herself isolated. Her own parents, who could not be visited too frequently, might have little apparent sympathy as they were part of the 'contract' which was the basis of the marriage.

Despite our wide network of health centres and clinics, there were still large gaps, leaving some villagers a long distance to walk for any kind of health care. To bridge the gaps, smaller units (*postes d'animation*) were created to serve smaller communities. Amoti taught the new village health workers (*animateurs*) the basics of health and hygiene. It was their job to record births and deaths in the village and visit homes to teach and encourage the families. They were responsible for teaching the digging and maintenance of latrines and protected water supplies.

The infrastructure and supervision of the health posts and the training of the health workers needed careful planning. Each village was responsible for the choice of their health workers, built their health huts (*postes d'animation*), and appointed their village health committee. It was encouraging to see new developments in the work, and the village health workers' quality of care and enthusiasm in improving the health of their communities was impressive. Achieving a certain level of health and hygiene in the village won a health flag for the village, which was presented by the Chief of the Collectivity and was proudly flown from the roof of the health hut.

Amoti had 22-year-old identical twins, Nyangoma and Nyakato (their names being, respectively, first- and second-born twin girls). The twins were among the few local girls to complete their school education.

Nyangoma helped the health team, and Nyakato the development team. Both girls showed leadership skills, and were given work that matched their skills, but lacked professional training. Later, Nyangoma became a nurse, qualifying with a state diploma at Boga, and went on to gain a Master's degree in Community Health at the Liverpool School of Tropical Medicine. Nyakato began a path towards development studies, but tragically died suddenly during her studies, the cause proving to be a congenital kidney abnormality which she shared with Nyangoma. With treatment, Nyangoma survived two more years. Their deaths took from the development and health programmes two very special people, committed as Christians, and gifted as leaders. As friends, their encouragement, support and affection were incomparable.

## Culture

Eight months after my arrival in Boga, Amoti told me to expect some visitors. There was no explanation, but this is not unusual. I prepared some tea and put out mats for people to sit on. In the late afternoon, I saw a line of women coming down the hill, all in bright traditional clothes and many carrying fruit and vegetables on their heads. They presented me with gifts of fruit, chicken, eggs and other food-stuffs, and a new local 'outfit' in blue and gold. We chatted for a while and drank tea, and then the women, led by Amoti, prayed for me, and for the health work at Boga.

They thanked God for bringing me to them as a friend and sister. Then they welcomed me into the tribe, giving me the name of Amoti, since this is the 'mpako' of my key colleague and friend. I was overwhelmed by the honour given to me. Being included in the tribe gave me responsibilities which I was keen to honour. However, I was anxious that I should not be so identified with the Hema tribe that I had no clear relationship with the neighbouring Ngity. For this reason I started to learn at least greetings in Kingity and made friends with some Ngity leaders.

## Kisembo dies of a lack of peace

It was late one evening when a little boy called Kisembo was brought into hospital with severe kwashiorkor (an acute protein-calorie deficiency). He was two-and-a-half years old and I had frequently seen him in the pre-school clinics where children are weighed, parents taught and immunisations are given. But, as I reflected on recent clinics, I had not seen Kisembo for a while. Machosi, his mother, explained that a few months ago she had started to attend ante-natal clinic, and it was too much to come with Kisembo. Then she had had her second child, and was bringing him, rather than Kisembo, to the pre-school clinic.

The following morning, when I walked into the hospital, Machosi was sitting with Kisembo in her arms, weeping quietly. He had just died. As Machosi carried his little body out of the hospital, I walked with her with a mixture of hurt pride and compassion. Pride because I had failed, yet again, to save a child with preventable malnutrition, and compassion, because I could feel the pain of a caring mother. 'Why didn't you come to the hospital when Kisembo was first ill?' I asked. 'He was not ill,' was the reply. 'He had lost his peace.' I felt Machosi's wisdom and felt she was offering me a key to unlock the local understanding of health and healing.

Later that day I went to Kisembo's funeral because I wanted to begin to use the key that Machosi had offered me. I made friends with the family, and asked Chief Kisembo what Machosi had meant, in saying that he had died of a lack of peace. He did not know, but he, with Nyangoma Kabarole and myself began an eighteen-month research on what 'health, healing, wholeness, death and disability' meant to this culture.

From this experience I learned a Hema word which has come to mean so much to me: *Obusinge* – that which encapsulates the whole of life.[5] Machosi was saying that Kisembo had lost his Obusinge, his peace and wholeness. He did not die because of malnutrition or illness. From Kisembo's death, I learned to turn to the wise people of communities before depending on my books or medical knowledge and experience. If Kisembo had died from a lack of peace, then health care would need to include social, spiritual, pastoral and medical support. Kisembo's death pushed me into researching the local meaning of health and health care and eventually changed my professional life.

## Medical Boga

At the hospital, my early days at Boga were constantly hampered by the lack of facilities and equipment. For example, a forceps delivery required me to balance on the cow-hide straps of the bed to manage the procedure, and a patient requiring an X-ray would need to be flown to Nyankunde, at horrific costs. Within my first six months at Boga, both in-patient and out-patient numbers increased rapidly, and this was challenging for the staff who had to work much longer hours. Normally they would get through their work by midday and would then go to work in their fields. This was important to them as their salaries were insufficient for their family needs. Nevertheless, they showed enthusiasm for the changes and put their energy into them. The increase in patient numbers meant that we needed more substantial beds, drugs and equipment. When the villagers saw new equipment arriving, they crowded around the plane, expressing excitement and thanking God for stainless steel equipment arriving. All the changes gave the villagers a sense of excitement and hope. They had had to manage with meagre facilities for too long. By August 1983, the first part of the hospital extension had been completed by Tim Rous, CMS, and his building team.

## Kisangani

Being responsible for the Anglican Church's health care throughout the country meant a lot of travelling. A 700km journey by plane took me and Diana Witts to the Diocese of Kisangani which we visited to assess the health needs. From the city, we travelled another 200km to Yamafaya. Our first challenge was to cross the enormous, powerful and beautiful river Zaïre by ferry. The 'talking drums' were needed to call the ferry across to pick us up, and then we had to provide fuel for the ferry's captain to be able to take us across the river. Arriving at Isangi, on the other bank, at dusk, we were met by the Chief and the vicar of the parish, who were generous in their welcome and hospitality. We left an hour later, with poor headlights taking us through a labyrinth of small tracks, which had been chosen by the vicar because the bridges 'were not too bad'. There were several dozen log bridges to be negotiated before we reached Boolo parish at 10pm where there was another wonderful reception committee waiting for us and where we were given another 'evening meal'. As we left to continue through the forest maze, the 'talking drums' echoed through the night from one village to the next, announcing our arrival. Eventually, well after midnight and 144 bridges from Isangi, we arrived at Yamafaya. The Land Rover was halted by the crowds from this village, and we were made to walk, accompanied by palm waving and singing, through a palm arch and into the church. Drums resounded back through the villages, saying we had arrived safely! At the Archdeacon's House hot water was produced and at 1am we sat down to our third supper! At some ungodly hour we found our camp beds – prepared in the school office. They were a welcome sight. But I was beginning to realise that everywhere we went on that 'safari', I would be expected to heal or recognise every illness possible! It was a painful expectation . . . How did Jesus feel? How did he respond? Wow!

The next couple of days were spent visiting villages, giving hundreds of immunisations, seeing patients, and sharing many generous meals. Our evenings were spent discussing concerns and possible health and development programmes for the area, while being grateful for the amazing efforts made by the parishes in such a remote area. As we sat round a hurricane lamp, we were serenaded by church choirs until after midnight.

Our return journey, together with two goats, five chickens and a duck on board, was uneventful until we slipped off one of the many small bridges into the stream below. News of the drama spread fast, and within minutes a crowd of villagers gathered – some to watch, and some to help. Orders flew from side to side and ropes soared under and over the nose-down vehicle, assisted by many hands pulling and pushing. Amazingly the vehicle was on the road again with no undue damage, and we completed the journey with no more drama. Just before arriving in Kisangani, we stopped for a meal with a retired clergyman who had severe toothache. I did a couple of dental extractions under general anaesthetic (as I had no local anaesthetic on me), before enjoying the generous meal prepared by his wife. My patient slept well all night and I was a little worried until I heard how much alcohol he had taken before I gave him his general anaesthetic!

## New buildings

On Palm Sunday, 1982, Boga Cathedral was decorated with palms and banana leaves, and was full of choirs and village people. After the service the Bishop addressed the congregation, with Chief Kisembo.[6] Together they asked the community to collect stones for new buildings which would upgrade the Boga health centre into a small district hospital, eventually covering a population of 150,000 people. Promises to bring or buy a certain number of 'piles' (a given measure) of stones were made, and a new chapter of health care at Boga began. It was exciting to see the foundations going down, and to dream of space to work in within the next few months. Before too long Tim Rous' skills as a water engineer enabled him to improve the water supply by fixing 44-gallon drums on stilts outside each of our houses, with a hose poked through a wall to the bathroom. He and his team also constructed a tank on one of the highest points of the village with pipes coming down to the cathedral compound (including the hospital), supplying water to the new operating room. This, together with a new generator and operating lamp for emergency work, a new ward for patients, and a new office, enabled us to cope more efficiently with a wider range of patients' needs.

## PhD

In 1986 I was offered a place at the Liverpool School of Tropical Medicine to do a PhD, and was grateful for the support and encouragement of CMS and the German Institute of Medical Missions (DIFAEM). Focusing on the local definition of health, much of the research was done by the villagers themselves, to the extent that some of them claimed it as 'their PhD'. The results were as interesting to them as they were to me, since it was all about each community's concept of health and health care. For example, one village discovered that Maria, an elderly, childless widow, was existing well below any reasonable standard of living. Of course the villagers had seen her appalling circumstances as they passed the small hut daily, and some had taken her food and water irregularly. However, it was only when the computer printed a row of zero values[7] for Maria's 'well-being' that the members of the village health committee were embarrassed and decided to build her a new hut and to improve life for her. Students helping the village became very involved in the project and took it upon themselves to take Maria some of their own food every day. They adopted her as the nursing school's 'granny', and brought her by Land Rover to the end-of-year prizegiving and graduation in the cathedral. It was the first time Maria had been away from her hut for over ten years, though she had previously attended church regularly.

The work that was started by the PhD research changed the living standards in the villages. It was discovered that the local concept of health was less related to medical issues than to a peaceful existence and sense of well-being. A change in socioeconomic conditions was the only way that such a situation could be met, so each village established health and development priorities and decided how these could be met. The developments were monitored and, as goals were achieved, we watched how new priorities would be established. The climax of the research was a two-day seminar arranged by the tribal Chief, during which many development issues were discussed. It was a very exciting occasion, especially as the Chief had extracted from the research the three most commonly occurring health needs as expressed by the village leaders, and formulated them into a three-year 'plan of action' for the Collectivity.[8] These included village-level education for six- and seven-year-olds who found it difficult to walk long distances to school in all weathers and who therefore dropped out of school,[9] protected water sources accessible to each family in the community, and group agriculture to prevent crop destruction by monkeys. These priorities may sound remote from health care as we know it, but if children, and particularly girls, have no education, they will not be capable as wives and mothers of establishing a healthy home. If water sources are contaminated, the deaths from diarrhoeal diseases will continue, and if there is not enough food to go round, malnutrition will continue.

Our attitude to 'health care' was turned upside down, by beginning with the local understanding of 'health' and from there working upwards, discovering what the local health needs were and how these could be met. Here is an example of how it worked:

One village committee discovered that there were a lot of children with malnutrition, and that most of them had illiterate mothers. Illiteracy, therefore, was taken as being the main reason for the children's malnutrition. The village committee decided that for the present generation of small children, they could only encourage the mother to improve the diets of the children. Their main objective was to reach the mothers of the future by giving them adequate general education. However, their village was seven miles from the nearest primary school – too far for the smaller children to walk.

It was agreed that a patch of forest (about five acres) should be cleared, and coffee planted. The income from the sale of the coffee would pay for two teachers' salaries. Coffee was chosen because, as an export crop, the price was less affected by deflation than some other crops, the idea being that the cost of paying for a teacher should only rise in proportion to the rising cost of coffee. However, there was no money – not even for the seedlings.

Rather than miss a growing season, the land was cleared, and a nursery constructed to grow the seedlings on the spot.

However, the cash problem was still going to arise, as the harvest would not be ready for two years. The committee had planned to build two school rooms once the coffee was planted. Either they would have to delay opening the school for two more years, or find financial resources to bridge the gap. They were given a loan by the local authorities, which was to be repaid in coffee and cassava within three years. We could have saved months of the villagers' hard work and thinking if we had insisted on schooling for children, since the effect of illiteracy of mothers on the nutrition of their children is well known, but this would not have given them the reward of having worked it out themselves, and later having the joy of seeing the children at school. What we could not have done is insist on such village collaboration and initiative in meeting and sustaining the costs. Our efforts would have had a high risk of failure, while theirs was guaranteed to work.

## Aru

Aru is situated in the far north east of Zaïre, and many of its people had returned to the area after having spent years as refugees in Uganda. In Uganda a sizeable number of them had been members of the Church of Uganda (Anglican), but found no equivalent in Aru and so had asked the Bishop of Boga to form an Archdeaconry of Aru. This having been done, education, health and development were top of the new Archdeaconry's agenda. In November 1984, I went with Bishop Njojo on a Confirmation safari to assess the health needs of the area. I was challenged by the faith and determination of the folk in the Aru area. It was an extraordinary situation in which I found myself, speaking English much of the time (a reflection of the past refugee experience in Uganda of many of the church people), and having my own faith tested by the love of Jesus in their lives.

A midwife delivering a baby hardly gives cause for headline news, but for me, to be able to deliver the infant son of the Evangelist in the parish of Ekanga, in a tiny, dark mud and thatch hut, was an unforgettable moment for us all, and I was immediately accepted. The needs of the area were desperate, especially for women and children, and it was clear that one of the priorities was to build a health centre at Ekanga. There was support from the local Government, and the parishioners had plenty of determination. We were able to return to Boga with three potential nursing students, and they were full of enthusiasm and determination to learn for the sake of their communities, which had nothing. Within three months, 700 small children were being seen monthly by a locally trained health worker, and immunisations were given any time one of us visited from Boga, several hundred miles to the south.

## South Kivu

In January 1983, Diana Witts and I were asked to evaluate the health needs of Bukavu Diocese which then covered the sub-region of South Kivu.[10] Our visit included an interesting trip to the Island of Idjwi in Lake Kivu. We stayed in a hut made of dried banana leaves; were spoilt with generous and thoughtful hospitality; and were rowed round the island, from village to village, in a dugout canoe, to the accompaniment of six vocal oarsmen. We discovered lethal medical practices done in the name of the church; and enjoyed the enthusiastic congregations who were oblivious of their Anglicanism, but were full of the love and joy of Jesus. It was a rich experience and concluded by our being thrown up fifteen feet onto the deck of the steamer heading for the mainland. I landed on a pile of bananas and pineapples, but regained my equilibrium in time to wave a fond farewell to those desperately needy people. For a year I had been crying, 'We have nothing at Boga' (and that was true compared with North Australia, Afghanistan and Bangladesh), but then, having seen their nothingness on the island, I began to say, 'We have everything at Boga – what can we give them?' We decided that our best contribution would be to make available training at Boga for village health workers and their supervisors. As in other places we had visited, we asked the local leaders to choose a few youngsters they would like to be trained as health workers or nurses, and took them with us (impossible communications made it appropriate to travel together).

## North Kivu

Early in July 1983, I went to two of the Archdeaconries of North Kivu Sub-Region[11] to complete the evaluation of the health work in the Diocese of Bukavu. The situation was very different from that of Bukavu and the Isle of Idjwi where there had been considerable apathy. In North Kivu there was initiative and enthusiasm but in several areas the standard of medical care was dangerous, and the management of health centres non-existent. This rather frightening situation was the result of the church establishing programmes without providing supervision. However, there was a concern by the church authorities to get things right, and we were able to make recommendations that a supervisor be appointed before the appalling standards were taken as being the norm for Anglican medical care!

The Bishop of Bukavu asked the Boga supervision team to look after North Kivu, and we were able to respond by sending health supervisors as well as community health workers to begin measles and polio immunisation campaigns for thousands of children. Children in the area were at immediate risk from a measles epidemic, which is a killer in many developing countries. Both of these illnesses had been almost eradicated in Boga where we had, by then, a 95% immunisation coverage of the six most important diseases[12] for all children in the area. A refresher course was held for the staff of the twelve Anglican health centres, and three team leaders were asked to resign or come to Boga for further training. This warranted legal and church negotiations, but it was an important step to ensure that Christian health care maintained Christian as well as professional standards and values.

On one of the safaris to North Kivu, I went with Kiisa Kahwa from Boga. The name 'Kiisa' is given to the child who follows twins, and our Kiisa comes from an extended family with several twins, so with several Kiisas. Early in Kiisa's time with us as a student nurse, we discovered that she, like several other members of her family, had sickle cell anaemia, a serious disease in which the body makes sickle-shaped red blood cells – cells which are rather like a letter 'C'. Despite her vulnerability to sickle-cell crisis, Kiisa entered into everything with enthusiasm. Flying was not good for her condition, because of the altitude and reduced air pressure, but it was the only way of getting around in an area where roads are either in an atrocious condition or non-existent.

It was exciting for Kiisa and me to see how the resources at Boga could now be used to help the other dioceses. First we flew to the Watalinga area, to the south of Boga. The area is isolated by the Virunga National Park to the north and west, the Rwenzori mountains to the south, and by the Ugandan border to the east. Its isolation means that there are few medical facilities for the thousands of people living there, and there is little contact with the outside world. The visit of a white person attracted some stares, giggles of delight and cries of fear, as many children had not seen a foreigner before. Together with the Chief and the clergy we discussed possible future plans for health care in the area. The most important move would have been to build a maternity centre, and to put a midwife there. At that time, most women were delivering their babies without help, and the consequent high infant mortality was tragic. For Kiisa, it was an eye-opener. She had never seen such a sad situation and yet responded with innovative ideas and somewhat naïve, but challenging, statements such as, 'If my mother had lived here, maybe I would never have survived.' Recognising Kiisa's potential as a future midwife, this pulled the group together in deciding to go ahead with immediate plans.

From Watalinga, Kiisa and I travelled by Land Rover on a very rough road through the park to the Ugandan border where, at Kasindi, another of the health centres of North Kivu was serving the local population as well as those crossing the border and the officials and traders who served the border post. Kiisa's enthusiasm for bringing health care to all communities met a disappointing barrier at the Kasindi health centre. It was a busy place with all sorts of legitimate and illegitimate trade; immigration and emigration negotiations; and all else that contributes to colourful day and threatening night-time activities. There was an active church in the town and an apology for a health centre. The nearest reliable medical care was across the border in Uganda, with nothing for miles on the Zairean side of the border. I had been there before, and this follow-up visit was to see how the staff were doing with the new work protocols that had been given.

When the Chief and the community saw the competence of Kiisa, still only a student, they wanted some Boga-trained staff to work with them, if only for a short period. This would not be a practical answer because of the costs of moving families to a culture and language group that they did not know. Again, Kiisa's inspiration silenced us. 'Why not train village health workers?' she suggested. The Chief was excited at the idea, and offered the old Belgian Government post-house for an improved health centre. We set in place the training of village health workers, and took some local candidates for nursing training at Boga. Meanwhile we would send down some trained staff for short periods which would not affect their family lives.

That evening Kiisa and I went to our hut tired but satisfied with the day's work. I was particularly grateful for having Kiisa with me – a girl of a different culture from that of the people of Kasindi, but with courage to ask questions and with initiative to propose answers that we had not seen. That night we slept well, but were woken early by a banging on the door. An elderly Muslim villager and a young teenager carrying a baby were sitting on the ground by the door. They insisted that I should take the child, and bring her up in Boga. Her mother, one of the old man's wives, had died in Uganda a month after having given birth. The father, about 80 years old, knew he could not cope with the baby. For me there was no way that we could take the baby, and I expressed my concern. I was on a journey and had no milk or other provisions for such a small child. She was born in Uganda and I had no identity or immigration papers for her. Kiisa, so much more used to family difficulties than I was, came up with the answer, instructed the father, and an hour later was nurse-maid to baby Rehema for the rest of our journey. This included both Kiisa and me walking the baby around outside at night, in the various villages in which we stayed over the next week, trying to get Rehema to sleep. Sometimes it was just a matter of learning how long her bottled milk lasted before curdling, and at other times it was coping with colic. Rehema became a sister to Neema (see page 34) for the next eighteen years, when her family came to claim her. She was very much part of my family at Boga.

Work in North Kivu developed and grew. The staff of the twelve health centres worked hard and the infrastructure created for ongoing training and supervision brought the various health centres working within the Anglican Church to a level where they needed a senior health professional as a co-ordinator. We were fortunate that CMS Australia was able to send Dr Brett Newell and, later, a dentist. The work was growing fast, and the inevitable problems and discouragements came with the growth, but nothing could take away the joy of learning so much from a young student nurse living with her own health problems. Later Kiisa developed severe orthopaedic complications to the point that mobility became very difficult for her, but she never lost her smile, nor her assiduity as a nurse.

## The Institut Médical Technique[13]

We could not improve health care at Boga without having on-going training for the meagre staff and starting a training for young village people who had completed at least three years of secondary school. The training was done in Swahili (and was thus 'unofficial') and focused on practical skills. We started with a band of six students who did well, and soon proved their worth. However, they only met the needs of Boga Hospital and the local health centres. Soon the other dioceses wanted us to take their students – a request that brought with it the challenges of finding the costs of transport and board and lodging. Many of the candidates we 'picked up' as we made trips to Aru, Kisangani, North and South Kivu, and later to Lubambashi and Kinshasa.

In 1983 there was an evaluation of our medical work by the District Medical Officer, who gave a very positive report in which he encouraged us to apply for Government recognition of our nurse training. I visited other nursing schools to learn about the structure and requirements for Government recognition. It was daunting, but the Bishop and the church and civic leaders were encouraging and offered their help.

Because of Boga's stone-built secondary school's proximity to the hospital, the Diocesan Building Committee decided to make that building into the new nursing school, requesting us to build a brick classroom block for the secondary school on the other side of the playing field, which would be shared.

Meanwhile, our first two-year local training of nurses was reaching its end with all 35 students having graduated and being sent to health centres in the (then) four dioceses of the *Eglise Anglican du Zaïre*.[14] However, while proud of their achievements, I was aware that they were not sufficiently equipped for the responsibilities they were about to undertake as they headed up health centres serving up to 15,000 people.

In April 1983, the student nurses changed their pens and notebooks for paint-brushes, and set to work spring-cleaning and repainting the Medical Institute and some of the hospital. Tim went round with a bucket of cement filling in holes, while one of his team carried a hammer and nails as he checked door and window hinges. Eventually the great (and dreaded) day arrived in April 1985, when the Government Inspectors descended on us. From city life in Kinshasa to rural Boga they were able to appreciate the scenery but groaned as we crawled along the ghastly tracks that we call 'roads'! The Inspectors were impressed by the organisation of the Institute under the church's leadership, but they were merciless in their criticism of my administration! Miraculously, a mini-Pentecost released my French tongue-tie, and I was able to cope with most of the torrent of French, after having spent three-and-a-half years speaking only Swahili and struggling with French (the language medium for education in Zaïre). It seemed that there was so much that was wrong, but I soon learned that this is how inspections are conducted; and that if there are no criticisms, then the visit was not worth the effort. The relief and joy of finding ourselves a recognised Government Medical Institute, opening with 45 students, was tremendous. There were lots of congratulations and the Bishop was enormously proud and thankful. I just wanted to run away and hide for a few days, but immediately had to attend a meeting of heads of all the medical institutions in the region.

My colleague, Balikya, had been untiring, helping me through sticky spots, and coping with most of the administration, as well as tactfully correcting my French. He was so like a younger brother to me, and so the announcement of his engagement to one of the students proved a highlight of the term.

## Health zone

A United States Aid (USAID) health plan was accepted in 1985 by the Government of Zaïre and inaugurated throughout the country which was divided into 306 health zones (health districts), each with a population of approximately 150,000. The geographical limitations of the health zones were left for local officials to define and so, at a meeting in Nyankunde attended by all health personnel in the area, the Nyankunde health zone was defined. Each health programme lost and gained work as the demarcation of health areas avoided duplication, and prevented one programme having to cross the 'territory' of another. No longer would the area of a health programme depend on church ownership but on the geographical division of the health zone. The Boga health programme was to provide comprehensive health care for 75,000 people living in an area covering about 100 square miles along the western side of the rift valley.

Village health workers were the pivotal part of the programme. I was grateful for my experiences in Afghanistan and Bangladesh, and used previous successes and failures to guide our programme plans. The difference between my former experiences and the programme developing around Boga was that the Asian initiatives were shared with other church-related health programmes and eventually contributed to the Government's health programme, while the Boga experience was the Government, and church and state were one in health and education.

In Afghanistan, horses, and particularly my own horse, Foxy, were important to my work as a means of transport. In Zaïre, horses were very rarely seen. However, two South African students had purchased horses with the idea of riding from Sudan back home to South Africa. However, by the time the students reached Boga on their journey south, they were tired of riding and of the responsibilities of caring for horses in a country that knew nothing about them. They offered the horses to us, and we saw the potential for reaching the villages along the Semliki River, some 20 miles away, with a rough track descending 1,275 metres.

The horses were an enormous attraction to adults and children alike. Several of the staff quickly mastered riding skills, and I enjoyed being back in the saddle. Tim Rous became a blacksmith and managed to keep the horses shoed. Within a year, the horses seemed to tire of the heat and we tired of slow travel (the horses were coping with very rough and difficult terrain) and so we exchanged them for motor-bikes.

Each month the community health team went out from Boga to visit all the health centres and health posts. The track used was in a very poor condition, and in some of the areas it was more like rock climbing in a vehicle. Nyakato Kabarole, as one of the leaders of the development programme, worked on breaking up the rocks about 35 miles from Boga. She lit wood fires on them to make them really hot, and then doused them with water in quick succession, hoping that the temperature contrasts would crack the rocks. To a large extent Nyakato's idea was successful, and had all the men in her team amazed at her logic.

Some of the six clinics were held in little village schools scattered along the road. The reception in each village and the generous hospitality of the people was very moving. There was something of the reality of African life as we sat around the fire outside the vicar's home, chatting late into the night, interrupting the song of the crickets and breaking the silence of the surrounding mountains. The villagers were crying out for us to put a midwife or nurse in their villages, as some of the mothers had to walk over four hours to the nearest maternity centre. Of course, many mothers delivered at home, assisted by their mother-in-law or another traditional midwife. Sadly, the rate of maternal mortality was high.

In September 1985, Boga Health Centre was upgraded by the Government to become a Hospital and a Rural Health Zone. It took me a couple of days to wake up to what people were saying about a 'zone'. At first I thought they were referring to a civic 'zone', but then I was called to Nyankunde for discussions on the divisions of the Nyankunde Health Zone. Boga Health Centre had become a General Hospital, with a catchment area of 112,000 people. There was no room for discussion because the decision had been taken two weeks before, and was already operational. Apparently we had fulfilled the three criteria – a nursing school, a doctor (Christina de Wind – albeit not yet arrived), and a functioning rural health programme. I wilted at the thought, but the news opened a door to developing contemporary community health.

During the past two months we had opened four new health centres. Each one had a different atmosphere and ministry, but all made the accessibility of health care to villagers much easier. One of the centres was down on the Semliki plains, in an area which could be reached by road and boat by Ugandans but not by the local Zaireans. We needed to cut an air-strip, and with the arrival of the first plane many cattle people, who had been cut off for so long, received medical care. A solar panel on the thatch roof of the health centre provided power for a VHF radio, giving us daily contact with the nurses.

## Neema

Neema was born at Boga in 1983 as a fairly healthy four-and-a-half pounder, but dropped to less than two pounds during her first month. Both parents would certainly be classed as 'special needs' and Neema's mother, who had tuberculosis, never established a relationship with her baby. Convinced that the lack of maternal care, if nothing else, would kill the baby, we turned to the Chief for advice. Apparently he had authority to provide guardianship for any child at risk, and so, without consultation, he made Nyangoma and myself guardians of the child. Until then we had called her 'Pusu' (Pussycat) because of her plaintive little whimper, but requiring a name for the necessary documentation, and aware of God's grace in having saved her life so far, we called her Neema (Swahili for 'grace'). For weeks, lacking an incubator or other nursing needs for such a tiny baby, Neema was nursed 'kangaroo style' – that is, skin to skin inside our clothing, an atmosphere both warm and moist. Evelena, our senior midwife, had an abundance of breast milk for her thriving one-year-old, and shared this generously with Neema, affectionately aided by some of the mums in the maternity ward. Neema grew into a bundle of time-consuming joy.

Neema lived at Nyakabale with Amoti and Nyangoma, Nyakato and the family. Their home eventually became my home and I was able to watch Neema grow and develop. She was a delightful, outgoing bundle of joy, known to the whole village for her vivacious and attractive personality. As a three-year-old, she would dance at celebrations, and as a four-year-old she would sit in the cooking hut listening to Amoti telling traditional stories. At six she went to school, but in the next seven years never progressed beyond the third year. She was severely dyslexic, and there are no 'special needs' facilities at Boga (or anywhere else in the area). At fourteen, Neema left school because she was embarrassed to be still in primary school at that age. Nevertheless, she was a little leader: leading the village church choir and family prayers, dancing whenever possible, helping Amoti in the village and telling all sorts of stories. Puberty led her astray, and the attractive youngster became a challenge for us all. Her behaviour in the market place was deplorable and got her into trouble with drink and prostitution. Despite the war, Neema moved to the Semliki area, 30 miles from Nyakabale, to live with a very poor young man who already had a wife. She had a very premature daughter, Elizabeth, who died at six months because she could not reach medical help through the fighting. Her second child, with the same father, was born in 2003. He was named Apollo and we all loved him dearly. He spent most of his early childhood with Amoti, as Neema had returned home for that period. Graeme (named after Graeme Skinner who visited shortly after his birth in 2007), is the child of a new relationship, with Justin. Neema and Justin hope to be married before too long, but they will wait the birth of the next child, due in June 2009. However, on my last trip to Boga (August 2008), Justin presented me with a goat, marking his desire to marry Neema. He is a simple Christian boy and looks as though he will be a good father and husband. Neema has been a special and important part of my life – through joys, frustrations, and sorrows!

*To be added:* *Nyangoma has settled quickly in Eastbourne, and is charming her hosts by her humour and courage. She says that the other students have an easy time because they only have to learn English but she has to learn about life too! When 'pop star', 'movie', 'spacecraft' or even 'popcorn' comes into the vocabulary, Nyangoma has to go to an encyclopaedia to find out what it is all about.*

*May 1991: Nyangoma (my Zairean friend and colleague) completed her training in community health at Liverpool, doing specially well in her exams. It has been recommended that she apply to do a Master's degree in 1992, so we are now busily looking for funding for her. Meanwhile she is back in Boga, no doubt coping with the many problems awaiting her. She will be very thankful for the arrival of Dr Richard Montgomery, with his wife Hilary, and their three children. A second doctor, Nigel Pearson, will be joining the team in June, to help with community health in the Diocese of Boga for the next two years. Both of these doctors did their tropical medicine at Liverpool, so Nyangoma already knows them.*

*Another person who would welcome your prayers is Nyangoma Kabarole, the director of health programmes for what will be the Province of Zaïre. Nyangoma is presently studying for a Master's degree in Community Health here at Liverpool. In June she will be going to Nepal for the research part of her degree, which will be yet another change and challenge to face. She has done exceptionally well so far, and has adapted quickly to university life in England. She manages to keep my flat much tidier and cleaner than I ever do, despite never having met mod cons before, and makes a lovely companion.*

*Nyangoma and Pat in Boga, 1980s*

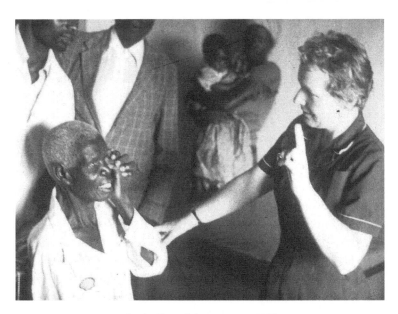

*Pat in Boga doing eye tests, 1985*

# CHAPTER 3

# Health, Healing and Wholeness

## Introduction

Higher studies at Liverpool School of Tropical Medicine (LSTM), using the concept of health from Boga as the subject of my doctoral thesis, brought me new opportunities. My commitment to the Christian healing ministry through CMS remained very important to me. Professor Ken Newell, my mentor at Liverpool, conjured up and offered an amazing job description for a mission partner. His proposal was that I have a senior lectureship at the LSTM, together with a two-year consultancy at the Christian Medical Commission (CMC) of the World Council of Churches (WCC), and continue as a CMS mission partner. Amazingly, it worked, and even more amazingly, all the people involved in the decision committed themselves to supporting this innovative way of putting together academia, experience and ministry. My own background and the experience I had gained in North Australia, Afghanistan, Bangladesh and Zaïre proved to be important pillars for the future work.

CMC was created to answer some of the questions being raised about the Christian healing ministry.[15] It was clear that many communities did not consider 'health' as being primarily medical, but more related to peace and justice, to lifestyles and spirituality, with poverty being the main cause of ill health. My particular responsibility at CMC was the promotion of holistic approaches to health care in Africa, which would meet the needs of communities and churches, and would be supported by local, national and international groups. The first task I set myself was to discover what had already been done and what there was to do. I launched out on my first trip, which included Rwanda, Tchad,

Zaïre, Cameroun and Togo, at the end of which I reflected on the kaleidoscope of events, which left me with two major concerns: one was about the quality of care given in Christian health programmes, and the second was the lack of collaboration between churches, and between churches and governments, with the inevitable wastage of resources. Some African countries, and particularly the English-speaking ones, had established church health co-ordinating agencies, which facilitated sharing between programmes and acted as a liaison between church programmes and the respective governments. The co-ordinating agencies usually made health education resources and drugs available at affordable prices to member programmes.

## Travel

Travel became an occupational hazard, with two British passports changing hands rapidly between consular offices and my very dependable travel agent. For example, I might be at a conference in Geneva while my visas, needed for the next journey, were locked up in an office in Brussels. Frequently, the travel agent would send all my travel documents to meet me on the plane.

On one occasion my name was called over the PA system. Apparently, by mistake, the BA Heathrow check-in staff had removed the Dar-es-Salaam/Nairobi portion of my ticket. They had telexed their Nairobi office who had issued a new ticket at an office a short walk away, but a walk which required that I be escorted through customs. The 'nod' from an official exempted me from questions being asked about the 17kg starter-motor which I was carrying for Boga!

The journey to a conference location in Douala, Cameroun, was an unpleasant adventure. The city was wrecked, with burnt-out cars and shattered windows of Government buildings. Burning tyres still littered the road where people had been killed. A few days later, travelling north, the flight was overbooked and I almost lost my seat as extra passengers who had been badly injured in the fighting required transfer for emergency treatment.

After a few months I was going back to countries for a second or third time, and had friends waiting for me at the now less-strange airports. I began to know airline schedules almost as well as the travel agent and the peculiarities of each country's customs officials. Between trips I worked either in Geneva at the World Council of Churches (WCC), or in Liverpool at the School of Tropical Medicine. In Geneva I was able to enjoy working at WCC and the beautiful city, and avoided most of the pitfalls and less agreeable aspects of the international jet-setter's life. Liverpool was always a tonic, with colleagues ready to listen, students to learn, and a church to support and encourage me – and my own bed in my own home for a couple of weeks at a time.

## Kisumu

There was a terrific storm and I was freezing. The terminal shook with vibrations from the thunder, and the lightning was fierce. I did not like the idea of flying in that weather! But I did not have to – the incoming flight had come within ten miles of Kisumu, but could not get any further because of the storm. The pilot hovered over Lake Victoria for half an hour, and then, for fear of running out of fuel, returned to Nairobi. I was then concerned about my morning flight to Heathrow. However, at 7pm we heard that the plane had again left Nairobi and would arrive in one hour. The storm had cleared, but just at that point all the airport lights went out. Imagine a small airport lounge full of passengers in total darkness. Then there was drama as a stand-by generator was sought, for the landing lights if nothing else. Eventually the fire-engine was used. Finally all the available vehicles were driven onto the runway with headlights and flashing warning lights on. The plane landed, and just as it came to a halt at the terminal building the lights went back on!

## Teething problems

The new jet-setting-gypsy-mission partner job had teething problems, and I had to make adjustments after the laid-back Boga lifestyle! The first six months were tough as I coped with a sense of insecurity, finding my way around in the international community, and trying to understand the work. Jet-setting did not leave much space for socialising or personal crisis, such as when 'Mum' (Ethel) Parsons died while I was in Bukavu Diocese in Zaïre. Ethel Parsons had taken me into her home and family when I was eighteen. I shared everything with her through weekly letters – which she returned to me each time I came home (often with spelling mistakes corrected!). The grief was awful – but at least I was with old friends. Africans have so much to teach Westerners about caring and comforting. Their love was abundant and sufficient.

## Geneva work

Much of my work with CMC was based on my former experiences, and particularly those at Boga where the community was discovering its own quest for health ('Obusinge'). From a CMS point of view, I was still under the leadership of the Bishop of Boga, and so it was important to me, to Boga and to the work at CMC, that we remained in touch and that I continue to learn from the Boga story.

The 'style' of most of the CMC team's work was to lead or support others in seminars or workshops, some of which were related to 'health, healing and wholeness' – the theme of CMC – while others were related to concerns of the specific country or region.

The World Health Assembly, held annually at the Palais de Nations in Geneva, brought together Ministers of Health and other delegates from all UN member states, and was an occasion for organisations such as CMC/WCC to catch up with and contribute to discussions on health policies and developments. For those of us representing WCC, it was an occasion to discuss the role of church-related health programmes in specific countries, negotiating on behalf of our colleagues, or lobbying for justice issues in health and particularly in primary health care. It took several years to master the approach (I continued to attend the Assembly on behalf of WCC for longer than the time of my contract) but it proved very helpful when visiting countries to be able to meet senior staff from the Ministry of Health and to refer back to issues discussed at the Assembly.

During the 1991 Assembly, the International Federation of Red Cross and Red Crescent Societies celebrated their anniversary with a musical 'extravaganza'. The plight of victims of war was poignantly brought before the Geneva community and its international visitors in a Festival of Peace. The London

Chamber Orchestra excelled in an outdoor concert, supported by spectacular stage-managing. The orchestra wanted to 'heal, inspire, illuminate and pardon' through their music. For the thousands of us watching they certainly achieved their objective. At the conclusion, as children sang, an Angolan boy, scarred by war, lit a peace candle and shared his flame with those of us waiting with candles to be lit. But I was left wondering . . . 'What have I done to bring peace and protect the victims of war – not just big wars, but the everyday ones?' In the office, in the lecture room, during my many journeys, during the brief periods at home, I am so involved with myself and 'my' work that I seldom make time for those poor victims – until, of course, I am victimised and need support!

The Boga concept of 'Obusinge', which carried the ethos of peace, was part of my being. Staying in Kumasi Diocese, in Ghana, as a guest of the Bishop and his wife, I was spoiled by generous hospitality, and tasted the excitement of a Ghanaian liturgy (even with Ancient and Modern in African rhythm – beautiful!). There was no rush, plenty of time to talk and share; time to look and learn and time to give and receive. The Mothers' Union groups in the town supporting their poorer sisters in the villages; a town parish adopting a rural cousin parish, where mutual support was the essence of life.

Most of the participants at CMC's workshops in Africa would have had training similar to my own and would now be holding senior positions. Yet the programmes for which they were responsible would often be serving poor communities in which healthy living was out of reach. Unfortunately, senior health staff were often out of touch with poverty issues. One such conference, at which I was speaking and representing CMC, which was held regularly either near Nairobi or in an Asian city, was designed to maintain the academic and clinical accreditation of Christian health professionals, many of whom were missionaries. Christian academics from universities of international repute shared the latest research results and advised on modern techniques and treatments. The subjects may have been important to maintain home-country accreditation but did little to encourage foreign health professionals to listen to the local people and to work with them.

In Burundi I met and shared a meal with a group of professors whom I had previously taught in Liverpool. The one-time Minister of Health of Nigeria had strong links with Liverpool, where he had received awards. He and other former colleagues and Liverpool friends talked health politics into the night. I began to feel the dilemma of polarisation and even fragmentation for those answerable to the vested interests of political and professional extremes. They remembered my stories of 'Obusinge' and the anecdotes of responding to community needs and were convincing in talking about how they listened to and worked with communities.

Some conferences gave space for concerned groups to express real needs and show complete engagement with important causes. In August 1990 I attended a Conference for Women and Youth in Health, held in Winnoba, Ghana. A lively dog-collared lady in bright African dress danced her way up to the bowl into which the collection was to be put, and was followed by her equally vivacious colleagues. The same group enjoyed early morning swims in the sea, as I did, and paraded around the town to a brass band before sitting outside a mud hut drinking anything from Coca-Cola to the local potent brew while discussing deep theological themes – from an African perspective. I felt very privileged to share in so much richness of culture and spirituality, but was challenged at how we, in Britain, need to radically change our perception of 'mission'. We need to understand that we are partners with our African colleagues and that they have a wealth of experience and talent to share with us.

In August 1990, CMC, together with the International Federation of Red Cross and Red Crescent Societies, held a workshop in Bénin for health programme leaders. The participants had come to learn how to facilitate communities to identify and respond to their own health problems. Health professionals often think they hold the monopoly in health care, which makes it an expensive luxury instead of the 'right' of all people. Following the workshop, I visited some of the participants in their own villages. One such visit in Bénin remains a vivid memory which I shall always treasure. We spent a day in an animist village. The culture was rich but there was material poverty. With pride the traditional healer took me into his 'healing temple'. The village committee was in control of 'health', supported by a hospital some miles away. I learned a great deal about the village and the culture and, at the end of the day, refreshed by a slight breeze as the sun went down, we chatted, danced and sang with the villagers. Then a man climbed up a coconut tree and lopped off coconuts. We drank the milk thirstily, and then shared Fanta with them. Was I imagining it, or was there a very special kind of communion in that coming together?

One of the most exciting workshops was in June 1991, in N'goundéré and Mbé, Cameroun, where I was working with the Evangelical Lutheran Church of Cameroun. Chief Kisembo, who had contributed so much to the development of community health in Boga (Zaïre) was among the 30 participants, most of whom were working in church-related health programmes.

The workshop was designed to be practical, with participants divided into groups with each group relating to a village. They were learning to 'listen' to the community, but most of the village leaders decided that this should be done by attending meetings, which were decidedly boring and at which impressions given did not necessarily represent the needs. The situation was redeemed by asking the participants what they had seen and heard outside the meetings. Chief Kisembo, who was the most experienced at 'watching and listening', had already led his group in contingency plans. They had been watching the women of the house in which they stayed leave home at 5am with their hoes and return to the home around 7am carrying water and firewood. Without discussing his plans, Kisembo followed the women. In turn, he was followed by his team picking up some spare hoes on their way. He realised that culturally he was erring on a gender taboo, but knew that hospitality would pardon that. They did not talk with the women (language was something of a barrier) but just copied what they did. The women chatted and laughed between themselves as they tilled their fields. Then, at a certain point, they gathered together, put their empty pots on their heads and headed off towards a water source. At the same time, other groups of women from different directions were also making their way to the water. A much larger group of women was now together at the water source, which had clearly been visited by animals and which was filthy. Among the women were a few who could speak some French and, incredulous at finding a bunch of visitors from several African countries among them, started chatting. Kisembo did not give his Chiefly status away, nor did he say very much, but he listened and looked. Together, as though a siren had been heard, the women started to fill their water pots, say their 'Goodbyes' and head off towards their respective homes.

Now part of the community, a participant who could communicate with the women, started to ask more questions. 'Why do you take your water pots so far when you have a pump just outside the house?' An abrupt reply informed him that the pump did not work. 'Then why not have it repaired?' Apparently the women did not feel they owned the pump, but it belonged to an organisation which had persuaded the villagers that they needed a pump. Then the group of women erupted in laughter. By this time there was a growing relationship between the participants and the women. In a mixture of broken French and the local language, the women explained that if they took water from the pump outside the house, their only source of socialising with other women would be lost. This was a culture in which the women were confined to the home apart from their work in the fields. To meet at the water source gave them just a little time to share their concerns and news and to support one another. They concluded that if anyone wanted to help them, they would ask that their water source be constructed to prevent the animals soiling the area.

By listening and watching the villagers, the participants learned the mistake so frequently made in health and development, and that was that the professionals or agency leaders have all the answers (persuading the village leaders – usually the men who do not collect the water). When this star group reported back to the other participants there was considerable discussion. Most of them thought the women should have used the pump, but the day and workshop ended very positively. A game we had played to introduce 'listening and watching' which we called 'The Secret Box' was brought back by Chief Kisembo. He said that, as a Chief, the game had taught him how to allow transformation and development in a conservative culture. I was able to support him in this, as we shared how we learned through the concept of 'Obusinge' (that which encapsulates the whole of life).

The First Conference of Private Health Co-ordinating Organisations in Francophone West Africa brought together 25 participants, from ten countries. It was hosted by a Catholic organisation in Senegal, with the objective of improving the efficacy of church-related health organisations, their drug supplies and training programmes. They were committed to improving communications with their respective Governments and international organisations and with the communities they served. As I sat with the participants I ached with a longing for some liberation in their thinking. There were many health professionals from European French-speaking countries among the participants, who were institutionalised in their thinking by their religious communities. The situation was so different from that of East and Central Africa where there was considerable co-operation with governments, international organisations and with local communities. At this conference major subjects were discussed rather academically, but at least ten countries had come together and made a serious effort to collaborate. Again, my job was to make friends and to follow them up as they worked through their plans for the future.

## The cost of health care

During an Oxfam study concerning the cost of health care (1989) in Uganda, Tchad and Zaïre, anecdotes of the effects on the patient told their own story. For example, a Tchadian woman who was nearing the end of her pregnancy was found to have pneumonia. She had saved money for her delivery, but had not expected complications. If she spent the money to treat the pneumonia, she would not be able to afford a safe delivery. She had already lost children when having babies at home, without assistance, and did not want to risk a similar occurrence. Rather, she hoped that the onset of labour would soon begin, and that she would be treated for her pneumonia at the same time as having the baby.

A teenaged orphan in Zaïre had an injured ankle. She said that the people in the village were very kind to her, giving her food and shelter, but she could not presume upon their generosity by asking for money for the treatment of her ankle. She had put leaves on her leg to reduce the swelling and sat quietly in the shade of a tree, nursing the pain.

In Tchad, there was a considerable gap between the rich traders and poor villagers. The villagers were found to weigh up their priorities. Although in Tchad and Uganda medicines were relatively inexpensive, the cost and inconvenience of travelling to a health centre were taken into consideration. For example, rarely were villagers with the common conjunctivitis prepared to travel more than 5km for treatment, but they would do so for an incapacitating disease, such as diarrhoea. This was in an area where a village health worker (VHW) had been chosen, and a 'village pharmacy' had been constructed. However, the VHW would be giving out drugs, not attending to the fact that there were no homes with a latrine, no clean water available within 5km, and hygiene of the village had never been considered.

In some parts of Zaïre, villagers assessed the probability of a patient dying. Funeral rites are essential, but expensive. If a patient is treated and then dies, the expense becomes prohibitive, and the funeral rites have to be curtailed. This is considered to be disrespectful to the deceased. If, in the family's opinion, a patient is moribund, he or she will not be taken for treatment.

Paying for treatment meant that other factors were taken into consideration, such as the costs to the patient in time, transport, clothing, etc. Where village health committees had authority to plan their programmes, and VHWs had a few drugs, the poor usually had access to health care, but not to preventative care because this was not lucrative for the VHW or affordable for the community.

Some health supervisors expressed the concern that the cost of treatment dissuaded patients from coming early in the course of an illness. Consequently, the treatment required in the late stage of a disease was more expensive, and there were inevitable increased mortality risks. Many patients would first look for traditional medicine (which would be paid for in kind rather than in cash and was culturally more acceptable), and then turn to a health centre or dispensary when that treatment had not been successful.

## The training of health personnel: a university ahead

It did not take me long to see training as a real challenge for church-related health programmes, especially in French-speaking Africa. Most of the hospitals I visited gave good quality care and were training nurses to do the same. However, the training given, though the content may have been similar or even superior to that given by the Government, was seldom recognised officially. This meant that nurses could never develop their potential, nor move between employers. I developed a vision of having a university in Francophone Africa, using local personnel so that nationals would be able to study without the pain of searching for funds to come to a place like Liverpool. As I shared this idea, I was encouraged by colleagues from overseas, and from Liverpool and Geneva.

The conclusions drawn were that the training of health personnel should always be a priority for employers and that health programmes should allow a resource allocation for the training of personnel. Donor agencies should be solicited for funding for training/scholarships and a regional diploma nurse training school should be established for member associations. Other levels of training should be co-ordinated so that each programme could benefit from the others' experiences.

## Traditional medicine and modern health care

A pharmacist from Burkina-Faso, who had developed a practice of herbal medicine, gave an overview of his work. This was followed by group discussion on the subject, and visits to three 'traditional healers'. Collaboration with traditional healers was encouraged so that the richness of the psycho-therapeutic approach, with real sensitivity to the culture, could be implemented whenever possible in health programmes.

Pastor Lawson, working with communities in Lomé (Togo) and leading a Church of God Assembly, was an inspiration. Often I would see him walking or cycling around his 'parish'. He brought children together, enabled the women to speak against the injustices of society and brought the men into a rich fellowship of believers. Occasionally he would take me with him, but was honest in admitting that he did not want to give people a 'foreign' influence or they would not do anything for themselves. Nevertheless, he was happy to have me with him when he visited the prison, and showed me the system that he claimed had been inherited from the French colonial period. Pastor Lawson's healing ministry was popular, and was based on prayer. As I sat in with him, I was glad of the time I spent learning from the traditional healers in Boga. There were many similarities, although Pastor Lawson's prayer was poignant. Of course, he would be using the local language, unless his clients were educated in which case he would use French. Sharing with Pastor Lawson's extended family over a meal was a privilege. His widowed mother did not speak French but, like many other African women, knew how to express love, appreciation and concern.

Pastor Lawson introduced me to a professional traditional healer, recognised as an adviser to the World Health Organisation. His 'healing room' was in the middle of the city. Around the walls were hundreds of bottles – some containing potions, and others animal parts (for example, dead and preserved snakes, scorpions and beetles). In seeming contradiction, there were detailed anatomical posters on the walls, and a skeleton in one corner. There were plenty of old books around, and an 'office' area. The 'doctor' had some knowledge of a variety of healing practices, although his speciality was traditional Togolese healing. His excellent reputation with WHO seemed to stem from his ability to work within the cultural context using a psychological approach with a real understanding of the outcome expectations of his clients. He crossed any faith barriers comfortably and his patients seemed to leave his 'surgery' with confidence. He gave me confidence too, especially that a holistic approach to health care was very important, and particularly in traditional societies.

## The experiences of the Christian Health Associations

The delegates from the Association of Church-related Health Programmes in Senegal outlined how they had been able to co-ordinate the work of some 60 health centres. The *Bureau des*

*Formations Médicales Agréés du Rwanda (BUFMAR) Rwanda*, serves seven hospitals and a large number of health centres with a wide range of services including a pharmaceutical depot, a workshop for the repair of medical equipment, a community health education department, and a general co-ordination office. Both organisations represent their members in negotiations with the Government and donor agencies. It was clear that the experiences of Central, East and English-speaking West Africa were very different, and further advanced than those of French-speaking West Africa.

## DRC

I then travelled by road from Kigali to Bukavu in Zaïre. The roads were good and took us through exquisite forests and mountains, with monkeys dancing on the road being our only companions. For the next month I followed up some of my previous work with the Anglican Church. In the Bukavu area I travelled with Revd Bahati (later Bishop Bahati), a young pastor with a total of eighteen churches to look after, covering a very wide area, and including the Isle of Idjwi. There we met with villagers to talk about their vision for the future. They have no church (just a few sticks – the wall has fallen down, and there never was a roof!). The school had been closed by the Government because the mud-and-wattle walls and grass roof were inadequate. There was no access to appropriate health care so, with the community, Bahati and I worked on the idea of restoring an old brick building which could be used as a health centre. We met the King (or Chief) of the island, the Governor of the Province and other officials, appeared on the mainland's television and were interviewed on the radio.

The villagers talked of their pride in their village – 'because we were born here', and their sense of responsibility in wanting to improve the situation if only they had the resources. 'Why can't Revd Bahati stay on the island with us all the time?' they pleaded. With a population of 100,000 and five churches, there would certainly be plenty of work for him. But he had twelve other churches on the mainland, and his family to care for – all on a salary of only £3 a month! Tragically, while we were together on the island, Bahati's baby died. His wife had no money with which to find the help she needed for the sick child. The faith, the courage and the witness of that young pastor made me feel very poor.

Much of my time in Zaïre was spent with the leaders of the *Eglise du Christ au Zaïre*, the Protestant 'umbrella' body, and I visited some work in the far west of the country, an area that was unfamiliar to me. This meant hours of difficult travel, but I was able to see how villagers had involved themselves in all sorts of creative initiatives. However, the striking feature was always the situation of the poor and powerless, unable to take initiative or to attract attention. Despite Zaïre's major political and economic problems, there are some excellent church leaders in the *Eglise du Christ au Zaïre* (which incorporates the 64 Protestant churches), who are prepared to do what the Government is not able to do in the fields of development and health.

As I visited the churches and programmes of those who had attended workshops, I was often encouraged by the way in which communities were being listened to and watched. A Zairean Pentecostalist is an example. Feza, beginning to see what malnutrition was doing to the children attending her pre-school clinics, worked with community leaders to try to find the cause of the malnutrition. They were suspecting that their agricultural skills were not giving the maximum harvests (which should be three times a year) and so families were forced to sell all the harvest rather than keeping sufficient to feed their children adequately. Knowing there was a good Government agricultural training centre just over the border in Burundi, she recruited villagers and community leaders to join her for a visit. There they found very fit cows being used to pull a plough. With some outside help for the equipment and cows that were needed, the Zaireans signed up for some training. It took just a year from the time of Feza's inspiration to harvesting the first cow-ploughed fields. During that year, the health centre had improved nutrition education and child care, while a development programme had looked at micro-economics with the community. Through Feza's leadership, and with the collaboration of leaders and villagers, the culture was changed, and children had better nutrition. Additionally villagers benefited from increased income from crops.

Following the Ethiopian Evangelical Church Mekane Yesus,

many member churches recognised and affirmed the biblical basis of holistic mission. The Department for Church Co-operation report to the assembly in Dar-es-Salaam (1977) echoed the voices of these churches: 'Mission means presenting the whole of the Gospel to the whole human being. Evangelisation, diaconic services, prophetic witness to justice in society and mutual strengthening of the churches are all integral parts of the mission of the church.'

Today, this comprehensive understanding of mission is widely accepted. To make sure, a distinction should be made between mission and the related term 'evangelism'. Although mission and evangelism are linked together and inextricably interwoven in theology and praxis, mission has a broader meaning. Mission is the church sent into the world, to love, to serve, to preach, to teach, to heal, to liberate. This comprehensive understanding of mission is often defined by the threefold task of the church: witness (martyria), service (diakonia) and communion (koinonia).

Mobutu, President of Zaïre (1965–97) had a notorious reputation as a dictator, and as heading a country which was extremely rich in minerals, but where poverty was the norm. Zaireans often recited the 'fifteenth article' of the country's fourteen-article Constitution: 'Make do the best you can, with whatever resources you can find'. Despite Mobutu's corruption, some positive aspects of his leadership have remained in the memory of people, although these would have been in his own interest. The first was that Mobutu seemed to keep on top of tribal conflicts, through fair means or foul, and there was a certain amount of unity. The other important move was that Mobutu 'married' the church and state together in health and education. Any churches wanting to engage in health or education were required to follow the Government's protocols, and would be inspected to ensure this was happening before the Government recognised the programme. Once the programme was recognised, the church-related programme was recognised as part of the Government's structure for health or education. Boga is an example. As work developed, it was recognised as a District General Hospital (*Hôpital Général du Zone – HGZ*) with a nurses' training school, awarding state diplomas. Given that status, the Medical Director and Director of the Nursing School were required to follow the Government's guidelines, and would be frequently inspected to ensure these were being followed. These included the hospital's responsibility to take care of a marked 'catchment area' of about 150,000 people, ensuring the provision of primary health care. With over 60% of health care being given by the church, the system worked, though inevitably, not with an even distribution of health care and with all the problems that could be imagined working in a country like Zaïre. Nevertheless, it prevented duplication of services and prevented inappropriate health care being offered.

There are few countries that have similar relationships between the church and state as Zaïre, though many other countries recognise and appreciate the contribution to health made by the church (and other faith-based and non-government agencies) and have a relationship, usually made through church or other co-ordinating agencies (e.g. Christian Health Association of Kenya [CHAK] and Nigeria [CHAN], and the Uganda Protestant Medical Board [UPMB]). The co-ordinating agencies often act as a liaison office for the church-related programmes and ensure supervision, support and resources.

In Mali I visited a small Christian health centre in a very arid area of the country, north of the capital Bamako. It served a population of cattle-rearing nomads and a cluster of villages. The two nurses who staffed the centre treated those who were sick but had no community health programme. Their resources were very limited with just a few injections and other medicines. On an otherwise empty shelf was a syringe with an uncovered needle, on which sat a large fly. Within a few minutes, the lazy fly was obliged to make a move as the needle was plunged into a bottle of medicine, and an elderly nomad was injected with an antibiotic. This, I inwardly wept, was health care in the name of Christ! Of course, it was not just the fly that was bothering me. It was the whole conduct of the 'consultation' (an instantaneous diagnosis made without examination, and treatment which responded to the client's demand for an injection to help the pain in his hip, and so was rewarded with an out-of-date antibiotic). The incident had a powerful effect on me. First it made me appreciate all those who put so much time into making sure that the quality of care given in Christian institutions does represent all aspects of the

Christian healing ministry. But, second, it made me wonder to what extent churches with medical programmes are simply flying the church flag, rather than responding to the real needs of the community.

The Norwegian Lutheran Hospital at N'goundéré in Cameroun became one of my favourite destinations. I first visited there in April 1990, when, on behalf of CMC, I was asked to help the senior staff establish objectives for the coming decade. As well as getting involved in hard work, I saw much of the countryside, attended meetings, and even delivered a baby, while the staff at the health centre at Mbé were coping with an emergency. The little girl was named after me (Patricia Didi), and was brought to see me at each of my subsequent visits. At N'goundéré and the network of health centres supported by the hospital, the staff were very well motivated, in spite of incredible difficulties. Their 150-bed hospital had a good reputation and was clearly meeting many of the needs of the community. During my second visit there was a terrible road accident, which resulted in five deaths and 29 people being very seriously injured. We divided ourselves into five teams, and together worked through the night. I was impressed with the leadership and the commitment of the staff. This incident was a tragic reminder of the vulnerability of anyone travelling on the roads in Africa. I got to know the staff at N'goundéré quite well, and particularly the Oumarou family. Dr Oumarou was the dentist, and had a loving and friendly family. On one occasion he took me out to his fields where we thinned the corn crop until black clouds came. Then we drove up to a lake which had formed in a volcano's crater.

The coastal road from Ghana through Togo and Bénin was lined with palm trees and made a very pleasant journey, with easy border formalities. When it was possible, I would stop off for a swim somewhere along the route – preferably in Cotonou (Bénin) where the beach was short with a fast and usually angry rising tide. The sea was always warm and just made to drown any frustrations and fill me with new energy. Unfortunately travelling companions were rarely those who shared my idea of a 'break' – but we came to terms with that by getting to know the best places for a good meal that allowed me to get my swim in too.

In Togo, together with the co-ordinator for Catholic health

programmes, I travelled through much of the country looking at health centres and hospitals, and meeting some of the Protestant church leaders. I took the opportunity of meeting with the Director General of the Ministry of Health to discuss how he saw the role of church-related health programmes in the context of the national health programme. The experiences were varied, and left me feeling very concerned about the standard of health care practised in the name of the church, and particularly in French-speaking West Africa. But I had to smile, and greet the villagers crowded round a television at a pub-hut on Togo's main road south. They were shouting 'LIVERPOOL' as they watched with as much earnest as those at Anfield, over 3,000 miles away. By chance I witnessed, with them, Liverpool scoring a goal. I was suddenly the guest of honour in this extraordinary situation, blessed with cool drinks, and learning more about the health picture in Togo than all my meetings with political and church leaders!

Agu Gare Presbyterian Hospital was a typical 'mission hospital'. Missionaries from America and Europe took the leadership roles, and passed their expertise to national leaders of various levels of training. There were two national doctors and a large team of locally trained nurses, but none recognised by the State. The hospital was clean, and the care and treatment were valued by the local population. Agu Gare was one of the few hospitals that I visited in Togo that had a network of primary health-care clinics supported by the hospital. Children's growth was monitored, and ante-natal and post-natal care was given. It was a system I knew well, and taught at Liverpool. My frustration, however, as in so many similar situations throughout the developing world, was the lack of engagement with the communities being served and so the community had no motivation to develop healthy lifestyles which would become part of their own culture. It all remained very foreign.

Togo is a tiny country (like Bénin), which has a relatively efficient health infrastructure, but where some private or church-related European or American practices make health care inappropriate to the needs of the people. It was in Togo that I found some brave villagers, together with a Togolese consultant, Jean Pierre, who were determined to eradicate guinea worm from their area. Guinea worm would be easy to eliminate if people did not walk in infested water at water sources, and if their drinking water was filtered. Their programme was successful because they were able to describe to their fellow villagers in a culturally acceptable way how to break the cycle. Many of the local population had suffered the severe pain and chronic cohabitation of the guinea worm, which they could only get rid of by daily tightening the worm round a pencil or similar object. Doctors were seldom able to convince the community to change their habits, but then the doctors saw patients, not the community as a whole. Policy-makers talked finance and obligation, which was not community-friendly. Church leaders brought evangelism and a sense of guilt into the bargain. The Christian consultant, himself from the area, was able to speak in the local language, from experience of having had guinea worm infection, and with the authority of a higher education. As he squatted on the mat, drinking tea with the community leaders, he drew pictures in the sand. What audacity foreigners have to think they know better than Jean Pierre and his colleagues.

Though small, Togo is quite a well-established country, and so I was particularly distressed at some of the 'aid' in the form of milk powder and medicines that was being sent for 'missions'. Milk 'aid' for babies that should be breast fed went alongside a major international milk issue. Nestlé were advertising their baby milk products throughout the lesser-resourced countries, and particularly in African cities. Mothers saw the advertisements of bouncing babies along the roadside and wanted their babies to look as well as those on the boards. It seemed simple – mixing some powder with water – obviously those babies were doing better than their own who were breast fed. They had fallen for the Nestlé propaganda, but worse, because they could not read the instructions, and could not afford much powder, they just made the solution look 'white'. They had no facilities for sterilising baby bottles, and the water used for the mixture was usually anything but clean. Flies would frequently sit on the uncovered teat. The end result is well documented as 'the baby killer'[16] which eventually caused some churches, such as the Church of England, to boycott Nestlé products. While CMC fought Nestlé in European courts, those of us able to talk with senior politicians and health leaders in countries such as Togo and Bénin did so at every opportunity. A few years later I was delighted to find that the Governments of Togo and Bénin had banned the propaganda and that church-related programmes were among those promoting healthier baby care.

In Bénin I discovered the relevance of African Independent Churches to the well-being and ongoing development of the community. Pastor Mikael of the Church of the Holy Spirit, between Cotonou and Porto Novo, invited me to attend his church. It was along the coastal plain so we approached it by canoe, motor-bike and foot – a journey of two hours. Having left after an early breakfast (more like lunch) at 6am, it was already very hot before we reached the full church. The service had started and there was lusty singing coming from the large patchwork tent of a church. As we walked in, we squeezed between the hundreds of people dancing and waving. I was the only foreigner in sight, but no one took any notice of me. Rather, they were enwrapped by the Holy Spirit, with swooning and crying, hugging and anointing. Despite my lack of experience of such a scene, I was not uncomfortable. There was an abundance of love in the tent as the folk ministered to one another. Mikael spoke in the local language but had left me with a colleague who translated into French for me. The 'sermon' went on for a couple of hours, but was profoundly moving and made a lot of sense as Mikael tried to bring balance back into people's lives. A time of healing followed, with several pastors anointing and sharing with the large numbers of people who came forward. A pause for lunch was like a bumper parish 'picnic', and was followed by a rest in the shade for some, and a further consultation for healing for others, including an opportunity to see a 'doctor' (a loose definition covering a breadth of health professionals). Early afternoon took everyone back into the tent for worship and sharing 'bread' together. Mikael and I left in the late afternoon, reaching Cotonou before dark.

For a number of years, CMC had been working with WHO and other organisations to establish a protocol for the correct use of a limited number of generic drugs, rather than having a large array of mostly unimportant and non-generic medicines for which one pays more for the carton and trade name than for the actual drug.

Many well-meaning organisations and churches send out medical samples or free gifts to their 'partner' churches, which perpetuates the problem of health workers over-prescribing and making health care expensive to the patient. Food subsidies may cause unnecessary dependence, rather than encouraging people to improve their lifestyle.

## Nigeria

In October 1991 I had my first experience of internal flights from Lagos airport. I left for the domestic airport several hours before the flight because seats are given on a 'first come, first served' basis. We bought the tickets (and tipped the seller), paid our airport tax (and tipped the collector – tips are as frequent as breaths taken here!) and waited in a dull lounge with every conceivable cheap toy, confectionery and newspaper on sale, and more being pressed upon patient passengers by tireless pedlars. There were no signs up, and no indication of which of the planes outside was which. Suddenly there was a surge for the doors. I joined the crowd, though I had no idea if there was a fire, a bomb, or a departing flight! In fact, there were several flights, but no one knew which was which. We walked around three DC3s, all with engines roaring. I tried shouting 'Is this the plane for Jos?' 'No, try the next one,' was the reply. At last I found the right plane, which was lacking in safety and security, I thought, but then I'm not used to living in a country of 120 million people all wanting to go somewhere! The flight was good, despite the loose wires, the torn carpet, and the broken seats and seat-belts! We ate dry bread and drank juice from a squashed packet. At Jos we were met by Moses, with whom I studied and graduated at Liverpool, and who is now one of the leaders of the Christian Health Association of Nigeria (CHAN). It was great to see Moses again, looking grand in his Nigerian robes. Following a quick tour of the impressive CHAN office I was taken to my hotel to rest (in the executive suite) and prepare my papers, before going to Moses' home for supper.

The following day, having worked with Moses in the office in the morning, the CHAN driver invited me to join him for a trip to Zaria, about 350km from Jos (3 hours) to collect the President of

CHAN, a professor of paediatrics (and an Anglican non-stipendiary clergyman). The drive was very fast on the excellent roads (with painful pot-holes), but interesting. The driver was superb, which was more than could be said for anyone else on the road! I was surprised to see only white cows and goats – and wondered why they were all white. Spread out along the road to dry were grains of all colours, red and green peppers, pale cassava, red millet and other vegetables. As the number of churches became less frequent, the mosques increased as we drove north – but still brave little mud churches sat among the market towns. It seemed that even in the rural areas there were better housing and more commodities than in many parts of Africa. TV aerials could be seen everywhere, sitting dizzily on the mud huts! But it was still Africa, with women carrying everything on their heads, colourfully clad, and rich horsemen riding along the roads.

Wasasa, where CMS has had mission-partners for years, is part of Zaria city, so I asked to be dropped off there and was delighted to visit Meg Merrifield at St Francis of Assisi Theological College (and to share some wilting chocolate with her), and then to be able to call in at St Luke's Hospital – names which I had known for years. All too soon the car was back. The Professor announced that his brother had just died, so he needed to visit the family at Kaduna (140km in the other direction) on the way home.

From Kaduna we headed back towards Jos but, even on Nigeria's superb roads, it took four hours. The driver was very good and careful, but we passed a dreadful accident involving a truck and mini-bus. Dead bodies were still lying around, but the injured had been taken away. It seemed that there was nothing more to do. We arrived at the hotel at 11.30pm. I had nothing with me, since Moses had taken my case with him. Nor had I eaten all day, but I was too tired to go out with the Professor and the driver for a meal. The room that I was given this time was not the 'executive suite'. The curtains were torn and hanging from a string, the wiring system looked lethal and behaved temperamentally, and the bathroom facilities left much to be desired. Fortunately the bed was OK, though I had company which kept up a military patrol around the bed – I'm not sure if they were rats or mice . . . or both!

At breakfast the following morning, I was joined by the Professor, a former Foreign Minister, who shared his experience of diplomatic trips he had taken up the majestic River Zaïre on Mobutu's luxury yacht, watching the poverty-stricken villagers of Zaïre on the banks of the river. Later we drove out to the Conference Centre – a paradise for tired and weary missionaries, but very European. Unfortunately the 'paradise feeling' was ruined by a snake which had become caught in the wires from an electricity pylon which meant there was no power for most of the day. Other nearby pylons had been cut at the base some time ago by thieves wanting the metal!

The Conference was opened by the Minister of Health, Professor Ransome-Kuti, another Liverpool graduate whose health politics I had admired for some years. He is an academic, and a strong advocate of primary health care. To share a platform with him was a privilege. Dr Ann Philips, a CMS Salt Fellowship member, who, with her husband, had been in Nigeria for 37 years, was among the participants. I led a couple of sessions during the morning but then spent most of the day at the computer, with one of the secretaries, teaching her how to use the program.

The discussions of the participants suggested that working in Nigeria was all about working with bureaucracy. Those heading up church-related programmes do not have an easy time, and, while Nigeria is wealthier than many other African countries, the gap between the rich and the poor is vast. Most church-related programmes are still heavily dependent on overseas help and advice.

I discovered a hairdresser among the nuns present – and so benefited from a haircut that cost me nothing, but made a good friendship and enabled me to learn a lot more about health care in Nigeria. Back in Lagos, the CHAN driver took us to Victoria Island, the commercial and civic centre of Lagos, where the traffic was ten times that of London in the rush-hour – and it was Saturday afternoon! We walked along the palm tree-lined beach, and shared Liverpool memories over a meal. Eventually we left for the airport – a drive I will never forget. How can there be traffic jams miles long at 10pm at night? Apparently it is the same all day, every day. But our experienced driver knew the short cuts (as did at least half of the drivers, making another jam). The tricks included driving straight across roundabouts, instead of round; cutting across the grass on a dual carriageway and driving the wrong way blasting the horn; weaving in and out of the busy stalls in the market and trying to miss people; and not observing any right of way (if such things exist). I thought I knew metropolis driving from many countries, but Lagos beats everything! We arrived at the airport a couple of hours later. Moses gave me a book of Nigeria (no pictures of traffic jams in Lagos) as a mark of gratitude. I was touched. It had been an experience, and I was sad to be leaving so soon.

Once in the airport there was the same flight information (to London) that I had seen a year ago when I was stuck in Lagos airport *en route* for Nairobi. I knew not to take any notice, but there were no other signs at all. I walked round looking through the darkness for some sight of an aeroplane. In fact there were several. The BA one was parked to the left of the terminal, so I headed in that direction, and went through the security process. The first time I heard that this actually was the BA flight was when I was comfortably seated on the plane. I slept most of the way home.

At least Lagos traffic jams had character. British Rail's Network South East had no character at all on a Sunday morning. I waited three hours at Gatwick for a train to Eastbourne and then decided to share a taxi with a fellow passenger! The few hours at home (in Eastbourne) were busy and somewhat dramatic, arranging and re-arranging how I was going to get from one place to another, with my car lent to friends. By mid-afternoon I was off again – to Geneva to catch up with office work.

## Central African Republic

The Central African Republic (CAR) sits on the northern Zairean border. I was delighted to be invited to visit the work of the Evangelical Lutheran Church on the west side of the country, travelling with Norwegian colleagues from N'goundéré in Cameroun. Since we were on an unmade road, the journey was anything but easy, and particularly following several storms and with the fall of darkness. The driver and I chatted in French, and shared fruit which we bought along the route. The car radio was a menace, with broken languages and a cacophony of music, and, as so often seemed the case in my travels, we heard that the political situation in the country was not good. Arriving late at the Lutheran Hospital where we were to spend the night, I found that my driver-friend had a cold reception from the foreigners, which, making the journey frequently, he had anticipated. This was embarrassing after our friendship during the journey. I had supper and chatted to my American hosts and then had a good night's sleep. I hoped that my driver did also.

My hosts, Carl and Paula Stecker, made the priority introductions to the sub-prefectural (district) hospital officials, and this demonstrated for me how integrated the church's health programme was with the Government, to the extent that the church supported the Government's infrastructure. This was similar to Zaïre, and was impressive. Less impressive was the level of health care provided at the hospital.

We pushed on to Gallo, the Steckers' home, about 160km into CAR. The road was good (mud and sand, but graded) and the journey straightforward. The objective of my visit was to evaluate the church's health programme, but, as the Steckers both have a Masters degree in public health, I found myself speaking with the converted, which seldom happened on such trips. I was welcomed to the guest house, where I was staying, by a snake who was trying to get in. I *hate* snakes! At first I froze, but realised that did not help. A kindly watchman came to my help and killed the snake with one swipe of his hatchet.

The next evening I sat on the dirt floor of a shelter, in which had been put up a camp bed. There were no chairs, but I had a little lamp balanced on the bed. The hut was a little like a menagerie, with all the insects keeping me company – in fact it was so reminiscent of my former days of village work in Zaïre, that I felt quite at home. The 'bathroom' was improvised to give me some privacy. It was in a broken-down prison, with only darkness offering any privacy. I did a conjuring trick with my plastic basin on the floor, and then ventured through the village to look for a 'loo'. I found an enclosed area with a hole – and was very grateful that it was dark and I could only smell the condition of these 'facilities'! A nice clean bush would have been better. So to bed, to the music of crickets, cows, goats . . . and the suspicion that there were more than cockroaches sharing my little shelter. I was able to dispense with the scorpion. Soon after going to bed there was a furious storm. I thought the roof would come off, but in the end there were only a few wet patches on the bed. The rain was so noisy on the tin roof that it was like standing under the Niagara Falls. For breakfast we had pork (and skin and innards – ugh!) and cassava, black coffee and local doughnuts. By 7.30am we were at a meeting of the local pharmacy committee. It was interesting to see all the same tricks in a different context (déjà vu – at Boga and elsewhere). But the idea of village pharmacies is a good one. The pharmacy earns money for the villagers to spend on other necessary health needs. They have a Muslim in charge of the money . . . 'because Muslims are more honest'!

Church on Sunday was a lively interlude to the evaluation, with a 2½-hour service, during which time there were nineteen baptisms and an interesting Communion service. Members who had paid their 'dues' were called up to receive Communion by name, while those who were excommunicated (half of the congregation, mostly for adultery) left; and the rest received Communion at the end (gathering up the crumbs from under the table?).

After lunch I read about the history and background of the Gallo programme, while others had a 'siesta', and then left with Carl and a colleague for the 'bush'. On the way I learned a lot about the area and this interesting programme. At Foh, a village of about 2,000 people, the village development committee welcomed us, and I was expected to talk to them about health and development (sadly they were used to being taught, and I insisted that I was there to learn, but we came to a happy compromise by having a couple of hours interaction, and finishing with a festive meal and wonderful local music).

A visit to the health centre showed a brave, but very unsatisfactory attempt at health care. The 'doctor' had never had any training, but was coping with situations that would be referred to consultants at home. These untrained 'doctors' had been employed by the Government. There were also traditional birth attendants (granny midwives) working in collaboration with the centre.

Despite all the work Carl and Paula had put into working with the community, the church leaders were putting considerable pressure on them for more buildings. Clearly they, like so many in similar situations, wanted visible structures which would give their church credibility. It was an understandable expectation and would usually be an investment, but, by seeing this as a priority, they failed to see the sustainability of a community approach.

The staff at the Government hospital, in a French military base which the local leaders invited us to visit, were on strike, but a German missionary family stepped in and were generous in their hospitality. They lived in a palatial home with a wonderful view of the small town and countryside. Their home was of a prefabricated material which, with the furniture, had been imported from Denmark. The message given by this leaves us defenceless when the local leaders ask for money to build a maternity centre!

In CAR, as in so many countries, there is a fight to immunise as many mothers and children as possible, without considering the other risks to the child, and the fact that the child's health depends on much more than immunisations. This was typified by a child with serious malnutrition, whose problems were probably more related to the social situation of the family than illness. The team understood when I explained, but did not know how to get out of the trap they had laid for themselves.

### Visit to the south east of CAR

I was grateful to receive an invitation to travel to the east of CAR, which was easily reached from north-east Zaïre, to evaluate the health programme of the church established through the Africa Inland Mission (AIM). In the six-seater Cessna plane there were two AIM pilots (one visiting), one wife and myself plus 50kg of vegetables, meat, a month's worth of mail and parcels. The flight took just over three hours from Bunia (Zaïre). We landed at a military base in Zemio to clear customs, and then it was just a hop over the trees to the Mission. Facilities were basic and comfortable. The staff felt they had many problems, and they were particularly concerned for the time, apparently quite imminent, when there would no longer be missionaries to lead the health programme. The previous year (1990), eleven experienced missionaries left (not all health personnel), leaving just three single nurses between the three stations, and the pilot and his family.

The network of health posts depended heavily on the commitment of the health workers, trained to cope with basic problems and paid very little, with no hope of promotion or further training. They clearly had problems they wished to discuss. One of the major issues was that they were working in a voluntary capacity, and, although they had agreed to this when they were recruited, they had not expected that the arrangement would continue indefinitely. The whole issue of using voluntary health workers has provoked as many problems as it has solved throughout Africa. Payment is a key problem because it illustrates the sort of cross-cultural confusion that foreigners can get into. Most missionaries come from cultures where voluntary work is respected, but those are cultures where pensions and various allowances, as well as adequate salaries, exist. To the African villager, an offer of training and employment as a volunteer usually means, to the potential volunteer, that a salary would be forthcoming in due course. When it still has not arrived after a period of time, maybe years, in spite of apparently good work, there is confusion, hurt feelings, and eventually a loss of confidence. After all, foreigners, and even missionaries, represent the rich world. What does this say about the church? The idea of voluntary health workers came from China (the Barefoot Doctor) but the politics behind the concept would never fit African politics or culture. The Christian Medical Commission encouraged a re-think of the 'cheap labour' in church-related health programmes, but the injustice continued, and was more likely to come to an end by the collapse of programmes when foreign missionaries left or when the volunteers exploited their excellent training and experience by taking other jobs in the health sector.

The hospital at Zemio also had major problems. There were no trained nurses, but a couple of pastors had learned how to do some emergency surgery, and operated several times a week. One pastor did a Caesarean section on his wife the previous year – a familiar job for him – but tragically she died a few days later. The information system is very inaccurate, and the treatments given alarmed me. However, the laboratory work was good, and the hospital obviously had a good reputation – probably because it was the best for hundreds of miles!

Over the Zairean/CAR border, Don, the pilot, dived low. He

had spotted some elephants. We circled dizzily, taking photos of a family of them. They were an unusual sandy colour (probably from the red dust) – mum, dad and three kids. We then saw some buffalo, but by then a fellow-passenger resorted to more 'dramamine' tablets, so the fun that the rest of us were having had to stop, and we cruised to a smoother 7,500ft altitude.

## Visit to Bébalem Hospital – Tchad

One of the earliest visits I made was to Tchad, on behalf of Oxfam, as part of a review of the costing of health care in Africa. To reach Bébalem Hospital, situated in southern Tchad, the easiest route was through the northern Cameroun game park. There is an abundance of giraffes, as well as many other animals in the park, making a long, hot and otherwise boring journey very pleasant.

Bébalem Hospital was run by French Protestant nurses and doctors, mainly from Alsasse. For some of them, it was an accepted alternative to the French National Service, but meant that the staff turnover was rapid, and few expatriate staff members knew the local language or culture. The large hospital offered the highest quality of medical care available in Tchad, and its reputation drew patients from all over the country. The commitment of both national and expatriate staff was exemplary, and the generosity of those who contributed financially and in kind was considerable. However, the fact that such a well-resourced hospital was not working with the Government and other Christian and NGO programmes for the future of health care caused concern.

Foreign mission staff made up the larger part of the decision-making body of the hospital, and there was little room for local opinions to be considered. In the villages, under the supervision of the local church, there were some dispensaries and mobile teams giving immunisations and mother and child health care, but, against all international advice, malnourished children were given free milk. The standards of care at the dispensaries were well below those of the hospital, but some supervision was offered by the missionary doctors, who flew out to these small centres with Mission Aviation Fellowship. Such visits were expensive and had to be paid for by the dispensaries, but their income, dependent on local cotton traders and nomads, seemed to be able to cope.

Unfortunately, like so many similar programmes, no studies of disease patterns in the community had been done, and so it was inevitable that the leaders based their planning on the diseases they saw, rather than those that existed in the community. Some members of staff were conscious of the unbalanced approach with the emphasis on curative care, but felt unable to change the situation.

The nurses' training was unique in that it began with Bible training and then followed with a non-formal professional training which was not recognised by the Government. Few of the foreign health professionals had had training in tropical medicine.

## Tanzania

In October 1991 I travelled with MAF to Tanzania, landing in Dodoma where I was able to do some shopping before the two-hour journey on a rough but good road (bad for a Tanzanian, but good to a Zairean). We passed by a few small villages. The houses here are interesting – long, low and narrow, with a flat roof. Many are made of sticks only, but some have mud plaster, and some are built in sun-baked mud blocks. There were hundreds of monkeys on the road, some very tiny, clutching on to their mothers.

At Kilimatinde Anglican Hospital, I was warmly welcomed by Mama Rutha, the primary health care co-ordinator. We spent the evening chatting about the problems of the hospital. The main concern was that the Government recently stopped all its subsidies, and now they had to charge patients to be able to pay salaries, and pay for drugs and upkeep. Of course this is what most hospitals have to do anyway, but it is a shock when the community is used to free health care.

The night at Kilimatinde was a challenge. I sat up in bed, with a mosquito net shrouding me. Unfortunately, the net had some rather large holes (big enough for a rat to get through, let alone a mosquito), so I had to repair it by tying the net cloth that covered my water jug over the large holes. The generator was turned off at 9pm, giving a welcome early night. I had the essentials for the night – a torch and radio (to catch the BBC News).

The following morning Ruth and I drove to Manyoni to see Bishop Alpha Mohammed, whose diocese was only three months old.

The rest of the day was spent visiting villages – seeing pre-school clinics in action mainly under trees (over 200 babies at each one); looking at water-pumps given by Tearfund; talking to village committees and traditional midwives; and enjoying new friendships. Our lunch break was a bottle of Fanta and peanuts, sitting on a stone in the hot sand under a dried-up tree (the 'loo' stop was more hazardous, with only dry thorny bushes to hide in!). There were lots of animals around, especially monkeys, but the area is very dry and arid, and it was extremely hot. Apparently in the wet season the dry river beds become overflowing torrents of water, flooding rice paddy fields.

Back at Kilimatinde there was time to look round the hospital. Only about 45 of the 150 beds were occupied. Although the hospital is usually full, the Government's withdrawal of financial support, and the subsequent fees imposed, had led to a great reduction in the numbers coming to the hospital. It is a very poor area and health care is a luxury. During my visit, a meningitis epidemic had hit the area. I was able to send a quick message to Tearfund, who responded by sending vaccines immediately.

An excellent nutrition centre at Kilimatinde had had to close, and the kitchen garden which produced the centre's food, as well as the cows which supplied the milk, were no longer used. Yet that day in the villages I saw children of three who were so mal-nourished that they could not hold their heads up. In embarrass-ing contrast, that evening a feast was put on in my honour, served by student nurses.

There were, however, some important innovative projects. One village was making a reservoir (by hand!) for fish cultivation. The villagers were also trying to put down deep bore holes, but each time they hit salty water. In the next village, the women were col-lecting the salt, but what a job. They worked over hot fires boiling the water and collecting the residue under a fierce sun. Ten minutes with them was quite enough! I talked with the head-master, a village secretary and two traditional midwives about the general situation and particularly about HIV/AIDS in the area, and they helped me to see the wider picture.

## Berega Hospital – October 1991

About 500 miles to the east of Kilimatinde, I visited another large Anglican Hospital at Berega. A very bad accident two days previously, near Berega, had resulted in ten fatalities and 64 admitted to the 120-bed hospital. A child had walked in front of an articulated lorry, which swerved and hit an oncoming bus. The whole of the right side of the bus was ripped off, and then, as passengers rushed for the exit, their weight threw the damaged vehicle off balance, and it rolled over. It looked a mess. Although the hospital was busy, the staff coped in an incredible way. There were two doctors, a good team of nurses, and several visitors, including myself, able to deal with the injured. The way in which the staff and the community responded was incredible. Uninjured children of injured parents were looked after by local families, and food was brought in by the villagers.

That evening, as we all recovered from a very hard day's work, I spent some time with a CMS couple and a single CMS missionary, whom I had taught at Liverpool. I distributed the packets of soup and sauces and chocolate which I had brought with me, to the delight of all.

An AIDS study established by CMC was being used at Berega and I was impressed by the work of the team.

## Back at Boga

I jumped straight into a workshop when I would rather have had time to call on folk and to see how they all were. However, Chief Kisembo had arranged everything very well. There were over 40 participants, including some from Guinea (Conakry) and Rwanda, who worked solidly for two days. The organisation was incredibly well done, and the material presented of a high quality.

The workshop included two visits to the villages arranged for the participants. It was well organised by the Chief and Nyangoma, but exhausted the participants, who had to sleep rough and walk for miles. On the second trip, I went to one of the furthest villages, because I could not believe the good reports that the participants had brought back. I was delighted to find that in this village, Murgwanga, the work that we started five years ago had continued, and that there had been exciting results.

I was encouraged that this was the same in most of the villages. In contrast, however, the medical work had sunk to an all-time low! In Murgwanga, the villagers were trying to protect their water source, but they had no stones in the area. Because we were travelling down in the development programme's lorry, we filled the lorry with stones and rocks from Boga, and then we all helped carry them on our heads to their water source. Villagers were delighted. They refreshed us with the delicious root of a water plant, which I had not seen or tasted before.

One of the workshop days was spent with the Chief, who used his weekly meeting of tribal elders to show the participants the process he used for ensuring that people worked together in assessing needs and planning. This system started over five years ago when, together, we were looking into the local definition of health and at how the community could be involved. It brought village sub-chiefs and resource people together, with the Chief and the police commandant, to share the concerns of the Boga Collectivity. It is a structure which I have often used in teaching at Liverpool and internationally, to illustrate how health and development can be contained and supported at the local level. The sort of questions raised on that occasion included: 'How can we get rid of wild animals which take our crops?' and 'How can we get our market produce to town?'

Having sorted out the animals and getting produce to town, and been given one of the best of Boga's feasts, we were entertained for the afternoon. Wambuti (pygmies) danced accompanied by their forest 'flutes', and village people acted Hema tribal stories. Other tribal groups who lived at Boga contributed stories, songs and dances, but most of all they gave of themselves. Visitors were invited to contribute to the fun, and some did, bringing laughter to the local folk struggling with other languages but enjoying the visitors. It was special for Boga to host such an important Pan-African group, and the Boga community excelled in their hospitality and friendliness.

On the Sunday, the Bishop led a festal Communion service in the cathedral, after which the diocese entertained the 40 guests. I was proud of Chief Kisembo and of other Boga friends and colleagues. From their small and relatively isolated community they had allowed the treasures they had discovered about community health and development to be pulled apart by those who were less familiar with rural conservative societies, and were then able to reconstruct the Boga model with a rationale that defied urban professional advice.

I had been absent from Boga for four years but had remained in close contact, especially with Nyangoma. She had frequently asked me to work with her on an internal evaluation of the Boga health district. We planned to do this together after the workshop.

The experience of the evaluation was surreal. The journey itself was so familiar, but the situation so different. The driver managed the Land Rover superbly on the very difficult track, but often the sliding mud, ruts and rocks took him in quite different directions from the path he would have chosen. We reached Longba, our first stop, by mid-afternoon. Longba health centre had been badly neglected. The staff were ecstatic to receive visitors. The old pastor's wife gathered up her skirts and ran into our arms. The children (Neema and Rehema, now aged six and seven), who were enjoying the fun of the journey, were confused by the excitement, until food was put on the table. During the afternoon we spent more time reminiscing than evaluating. It was like old times. We had been through so much together, and then separated for four years without saying 'Goodbye'. Now, with the mud and thatch health centre falling down around them, and only a couple of patients a day (because of the price of drugs) the staff were at a desperately low ebb. No wonder they made such a fuss of us. Time went all too fast, and we still had 15km to travel before nightfall, which would take at least an hour and a half.

My heart ached as we slowly crept through the tall grass and mud patches. The driver knew the way even when there was no track to follow – as I did. Every bump was a joy, because it reminded me of the years of travelling that road. As of old, we sang our way through the hymn book (though, of course we could not use a book on such a road – we didn't need to, we had rehearsed the sequence a hundred times in the years gone by). Kids waved, adults clapped, and occasionally we stopped to embrace an old friend or colleague.

On the road was a dark figure. 'We've lost a shovel from the vehicle,' the man said. I did not recognise the voice, but there would be no other vehicles on that road other than the Bishop's which had left Bunia 60km further back earlier that day, heading for Boga. We caught up with the pickup truck, piled high with people, vegetables and goats, chickens and goods. We were in the middle of another storm, and so greeted our colleagues through the window as we passed. We turned off deeper into the bush as they drove on to Boga. It was already 10pm and they had four hours' drive (45km) in front of them. We arrived at Bilima among the hills, our destination, an hour (10km) later. The children were tired, frightened by awful roads, and cross. As always, some food inside them helped. We were grateful for the bamboo beds given us, though sorry for the nurses who had relinquished their beds and had to sleep on the cold, damp mud floor, wrapped in several layers of clothes. The rain and higher altitude had brought a sudden drop in temperature and it was cold.

The following morning, Neema was first up at 4am – but then she joined me in my bed, and ended my night. We started work early and then drove on to Longba, where the situation was similar to that at Bilima – a lonely team, fighting all the odds to keep a decrepit building open for the handful of patients who could still afford the luxury of medical care. I was so sad to see the state of affairs, and had to hide my tears, and keep up with, and support, Nyangoma. 'Why are there no drugs in the cupboard?' I asked the nurse in charge. I kicked myself. I knew the answer. The patients had no money for drugs, and the staff had already sacrificed their salaries to buy the little that there was for emergencies. What a mess! How complacent we are in our giving, and our understanding. This situation is desperate and no one is doing anything. I was beginning to hate this evaluation. I wanted to be back in Boga and show people that I cared by helping to get things straight again; by caring that people were dying at home because they could not afford help from a health centre. Unlike my visits to other countries, I didn't like being an evaluator for the health district which I had seen born. I didn't want to find fault with those who gave everything out of their nothingness. But they understood, and thanked me for coming. They killed a chicken for their rich guest, who left in a vehicle, wearing clean clothes, and feeling sick because she was 'rich' enough to be healthy. Actually, even the vehicle was not in good shape. It would not start and so we pushed it down a slope. But the rain that morning made it impossible to bump-start it and so it took twenty good-willed people to push it up the slope again. Four hours later it started!

On to Bunyagwa, where one of our old students was managing a health centre single-handed. The situation there was not so grim since most people in the village had cattle, and therefore had at least some cash. The little centre, built in mud and thatch, was in good enough shape, and the nurse had settled happily in the area with his family.

Getting back to the 'main' track from Bunyagwa was tricky. Rehema hated the 'rock climbing' that had to be done, but the driver was excellent. Often we had to walk to lighten the vehicle. Eventually we were back on the old road, singing our old songs, and sharing old stories. Two hours later we reached Maga, after more driving dramas. The village women applauded us as we passed by. We were among the Ngety, a tribe with Sudanic roots and an impossibly difficult language. Generally, they were agriculturists, often very poor but with a rich culture. Many were not well educated, except in some villages where there were secondary schools.

There had been progress at Maga, and the population had worked hard at increasing the number of buildings of the health centre. But still only a pathetic number of patients were able to come for care. Neema, tired of our chatting, and happy with yet another chicken meal inside her (the third that day), picked up the microphone of the humming car radio, and in a clear, childish voice, warned the folk at Bukaringi, two hours further on, that we were heading in their direction!

The road had dried out and we made good progress. An archdeaconry reception had been formed when Neema's warning was heard, and an impromptu meeting held. It was good, but the folk had so many major concerns. However, Bukaringi had made progress, and was offering a satisfactory health programme. Satisfied with more chicken, and loads of love, we moved on towards Boga, arriving home about 10pm. Rehema said it was the last journey she was going to make, and Neema began a long recitation to Amoti of all that had happened, finishing – 'but I wasn't scared!' We all went to bed, happy to be home. But I could not sleep. The poverty and desperation had really hit me. I had been away from Boga for four years, sometimes in England, often in Geneva, but for most of the time waltzing around Africa like a VIP, receiving amazing amounts of attention, when it was really all about listening to communities like those with whom I had shared today, and feeling their pain and poverty. We were in for another storm and it felt as though the windows of my room would break with its force. It felt as though the windows of my heart would break too. Had I been a traitor to these people I loved so much, or could our mutual love, which now stretched across continents and oceans, enable us to take an important message to the world?

The following day was relatively easy as we continued with the evaluation by visiting three nearby health centres. At Mitego we spent time with the Chief of that Collectivity, and at the last centre we were feasted. In the afternoon, back at Amoti's home at Nyakabale (in Boga) I tried to start analysing my work, and poverty kept shooting out from the pages. Devaluation was at a staggering rate. Since I arrived a month previously, the currency had dropped by 75%. That evening, we received news from CMS that, for the first time ever, some redundancies were imminent because giving in England had fallen so sharply. Amoti generously said, 'Never mind, even if people in England cannot pay for you, don't leave us, because we will always have enough food in the garden even if we do not have much cash.' What love and generosity the poor show us. I am so ashamed of being 'rich'. I was glad I was with Amoti and could share some of my feelings with her. She is a wise woman and her faith helped me to come to terms with being 'rich' when others were so poor. She was not slow to remind me that it was because I was 'rich' that many in Boga were still alive!

We set off at 6am the next morning to see more health centres – this time down the escarpment of the Rift Valley, to the plains of the River Semliki which divides Zaïre from Uganda. If anything, the drive was more dramatic than our experiences of the previous few days. Chief Kisembo sent a security officer with us since the plains were patrolled by Government 'operational' troops who were frequently drunk. How the driver ever found his way I don't know. We just kept ploughing through elephant grass. Every so often he stopped the vehicle to put water into the leaking radiator, and to take grass out of the engine. We arrived at Kyabwohe at 10.30am, and left passengers and the vehicle there, to cross the flooded plains on foot. The 12km walk to Burasi took us three hours – often in thigh-high muddy water, often falling. I ran out of energy before the others, just 10km of walking in the mid-day sun. I threw myself onto some soft (dry!) cow pats under a palm tree. Nyangoma and the Archdeacon followed me. Only ten minutes later I needed to rest again. Then I realised that there was pure salt on my skin. I must have been seriously dehydrated. In that heat, complications were not far away. We sent our escort on to find a bike, and we walked on gently. The 'ambulance' (a rickety bike) came to the rescue, and within minutes I was in the health centre, sipping milk. After a good meal and with the evaluation done, we had to walk back. At least it was no longer the middle of the day, so it was not so extremely hot, and I had eaten a meal and boosted my sugar and salt levels.

We completed the return journey in three hours, arriving at Kyabwohe at 6pm. It was dark, and we were scratched and dirty, but satisfied that we had managed to get to Burasi and back. We had been walking along the river bank, and realised that if we could provide a boat from Kyabwohe, the Boga doctor could get to Burasi at least once a month. There are crocodiles and hippos in the river, but apparently they are scared of outboard motors. The return journey would take only an hour or two by boat. As it was, nobody had visited for over a year, and no vaccines had reached the area.

We checked out the Kyabwohe health centre by torchlight and faced the homeward journey, content with the day's work. We sang as the driver began his assault on the elephant grass. Driving in the dark with no road to follow and very poor lights in a vehicle that had to be 'push-started' if it stopped, was, to say the least, precarious. We had several mechanical faults on the way, the worst being when the four-wheel-drive gadget jumped out of place on one of the back wheels. It was 10pm, and to correct such a major problem without instruments, and by the light of a torch, made the drama look like a film piece. There were fitting sound effects too, as a lion roared on the plains – something I had never heard before in that area. Each passenger then recounted a 'near miss' story of confronting the beasts. I was not eligible for the story competition, as the nearest I had been to one is nearly running over a lion's toenails in the game park, but that did not count because I was in a Land Rover.

Amoti had waited up for us. We sat with her by the fire as she bathed our sores and gave us hot milk. I slept very soundly!

The next step in the evaluation process was to meet with the 'wise people' of the Collectivity and gather their self-evaluation. These meetings, that brought back so many memories to me of when Chief Kisembo started the system and invited Nyangoma and I to join him some five years ago, always began with 'news and current affairs' for those who did not have radios (there were no newspapers in Boga). The evaluation then went on for over six hours. It was incredible what had come out of years of work, and how the Chief's trip to Cameroun was already paying off. Nyangoma and I left the group of 'advisers', and went to another meeting to appraise the hospital's activities. This took us until 8pm, when we met up with the Chief and all went home to Nyak-abale together, hoping that Amoti would have some food for us. It had been a long and taxing day, but very exciting seeing so much determination on behalf of that special group of the Chief's 'wise people' who wanted to put things right. We sat round the fire, sharing stories. Family prayers was always a special time in which all of us participated, from the smallest child to the oldest adult (a lady of 104 who had lived with leprosy most of her life!). It taught me so much. Neema prayed for my sore feet(!) and Amoti thanked God for safety, food and love, and that even in human-made contraptions, such as the Land Rover, we are protected by God's grace!

The next day, Sunday, I had promised to visit the local church – a small mud building which was crammed full, and which had an excellent choir with home-made instruments. There were fifteen baptisms (mostly adults) and a harvest thanksgiving (which, in this land of poverty, is held at least twice a year). We took a basin full of peanuts, which would be auctioned and the money given to the church. The service lasted 3½ hours, by which time we had to go down to the cathedral at Boga for lunch, since a visitor (from Rwanda) was being welcomed. As we walked down the hill, we saw a baboon in the trees, which attracted crowds of excited children and worried parents. Only the week before, in a village about twenty miles from Boga, a baboon had attacked a child carrying her baby brother on her back. The baby was killed and carried off by the baboon and the girl was badly mauled.

With baboons and lunch for visitors behind us, Nyangoma and I worked on further analyses and putting the report together. Sunday afternoons used to be special family times when I would play with the children and listen to their stories, but now I was here in a different capacity, and had to keep working. Nyangoma had planned yet another workshop for the following day – this time for the nurses. So the afternoon was spent down in Boga, planning the workshop together. That evening the Rwandese visitor came up to Nyakabale and we introduced her to fried, salted grubs (like chrysalises!). They were delicious, tasting a little like grasshoppers or shrimps, but our visitor thought that was a matter of opinion!

It was hard to leave Boga. On the way out of the village, Nyangoma and I were stopped by lads to whom we had been giving special attention over the years. Their mother, Gertrude, depended on prostitution to care for them and to buy the alcohol on which she depended. Gertrude's health was worrying eight-year-old Kisembo. She seemed to have pneumonia, but had no money for treatment, and had three goats to care for, the owner of which was paying her to keep them safe. We were able to get her medicines and organise some home care for her before we left. Amoti was already making sure that Gertrude had a meal each day. A similar case further down the road caused more delays. Because people could not afford medicines, they waited until they were desperate or dying before getting help. Eventually we left by road for Nyankunde – a six-hour journey, taking with us three children with badly neglected orthopaedic problems. Jo Lusi, the orthopaedic surgeon at Nyankunde Christian Hospital, was not only skilled, but able to make do without sophisticated equipment and resources. He and his wife, Lyn, were also good friends of ours. Lunch was on the table when we arrived, as was a pile of work. Jo and Lyn, with Nyangoma and I, had ideas for the future of 'bringing Liverpool to Africa'. That was our afternoon's and evening's work. By midnight my head was spinning with new and exciting ideas.

## Conclusion

There were many highlights during my two years of working with CMC. On the technical side, I learned a great deal about facilitating workshops to promote the empowerment of communities (i.e enabling health and church leaders *to listen to what their communities are saying* and *to work with them*, rather than telling them what should be done!). But I was constantly challenged and often depressed by the *injustices in health care* (church programmes working more for the rich than the poor; Western partner churches maintaining unreasonable control of African programmes; peripheral health workers abandoned by authorities yet expected to cope without sufficient resources). However, I was excited by the courage and initiative used by some health professionals to make ends meet and to ensure quality care. I was confused by church leaders who did not want to work with their Governments, and tormented by expatriates whose insensitivity to the local culture and priority needs led them to build 'white elephant' hospitals and health programmes which served their own interests more than the needs of the community. What a wealth of experience I gained during those two years, for which I thank God.

The challenges of church-related health care in many African countries, and particularly in French-speaking Africa, were numerous. The church is responsible for an average of about 40% of health care in sub-Saharan Africa (and 80% in Zaïre). Often this care is of a comparatively high quality despite the many constraints. However, all too frequently health care had been established on Western principles and implemented using Western strategies. So health programmes were often inappropriate to the needs of the people, and could not always be sustained without foreign intervention. In rural and isolated areas, where the better qualified health personnel seldom visited (let alone worked), nurses and health workers tried to meet the needs with very few resources and with almost no supervision or encouragement. The result was that fairly lethal health practices were conducted in the name of the church! The vision of bringing a Liverpool-type training to Africa grew and attracted the interest of academics, professionals and church agencies.

*'Does everyone have to come to Liverpool to get health care right, or can we take Liverpool to Africa?'*

*Pat in Bangladesh, 1970*

*Pat in Cameroun, 1990*

*IPASC's famous green truck,
Nyankunde, 1990s*

*Pat with Bishop Simon
Barrington-Ward, 2000*

*World Faith Development Dialogue,
2000*

*UN in Bunia refugee camp, 2000*

*Pat with Amuda, Bertie Squire and
Sabuni – graduation, 2004*

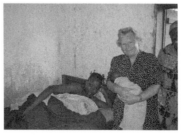

*Safe Motherhood Programme, 2004*

*In Sri Lanka post-tsunami, 2005*

*At work in Aru, 2005*

*Awarded OBE in Aru, 2005*

*Ordained priest in Aru, 2005*

# CHAPTER 4

# 'Obusinge'[5] Becomes the Cornerstone of New Training Initiatives (1991–2000)

## Introduction

'Taking Liverpool to Africa' was the next step, with the creation of the *Institut Panafricain de Santé Communautaire* (IPASC), based on the Boga concept of Obusinge (that which encapsulates the whole of life) and the importance of listening to and working with local communities.

## Personal preparation

How could I have prepared myself to create and lead an Institute able to respond to the community health needs of French-speaking Africa? My background was like a kaleidoscope of colour and shapes which had come together in ways that were completely out of my hands. Nevertheless, the experience I had gained in the triangular relationship between three agencies could not have been better. A two-year attachment to the Christian Medical Commission (CMC) of the World Council of Churches (WCC) and the links that this gave me into other major organisations and networks fitted into that mission, as did the academic and teaching experience of the Liverpool School of Tropical Medicine (LSTM), and the resources, contacts and friendships that would continue as long as I remained on the staff. Twenty years as a mission partner with the Church Mission Society (CMS) and with the expectation of many more years ahead meant that my interest in concepts and practices of contemporary mission would continue. Only a God with a sense of humour could have brought together the colours and shapes of the kaleidoscope to form a training institute for French-speaking Africa. However, where, when, how and with whom I should move on was still to be discovered if the dream of taking Liverpool to Africa was to become reality.

## Links and networks

I found that it was the experiences and networks of colleagues, friends and employers that had developed over the past two years of working from Geneva, Liverpool and my own Diocese of Boga (Zaïre), through CMS, that provided most of the answers. No sooner had I started to share 'my dream', than people approached me with more ideas. A number of like-minded individuals and groups had been thinking about training and looking for a partner. In some cases they had the resources but not the people, while for others there were people but no resources. Programmes in Cameroun and Togo were keen to be involved, but it was the Christian Medical Centre (Centre Médical Evangelique – CME) at Nyankunde, DR Congo,[17] which invited us to consider them as a local partner, while ICCO, Holland, offered funding.

Nyankunde, situated 40 miles from Boga and 25 miles from Bunia, had grown from a village to a small town since the creation of CME in 1966. Created initially by five mission societies, it had developed from a small Christian hospital to a district hospital responsible for a population of 150,000, with several specialist services, and a developing university college for health sciences.[18] In addition, CME Nyankunde supported, and continues to support, smaller church-related health services in an area the size of France with a population of some eight million; a service which is made possible by having the Missionary Aviation Fellowship (MAF) base for Eastern Congo, equipped with several small Cessna planes serving many missions also based at Nyankunde. Other programmes on the Nyankunde campus include an agricultural programme and a school for the deaf. Government-recognised diploma training was offered at CME in various subjects (nursing, dentistry, pharmacy and laboratory technology).

At the School of Tropical Medicine in Liverpool, I had been

appointed a Senior Lecturer, and later a Fellow, with special responsibility for the development of the work in DR Congo, which had, by mutual agreement, become known as the *Institut Panafricain de Santé Communautaire* (IPASC – which translates as the Pan-African Institute of Community Health). The LSTM was not able to offer its diplomas to IPASC students, but did allow us to use the School's logo beside our own, so demonstrating our collaboration in training.

The ability of CMS to accommodate my work with WCC and LSTM, as well as my engagement with other international organisations such as the World Health Organisation and the World Faith Leaders' Development Forum, allowed me to extend a holistic interest and role in mission. Associations within this wide network of work were not always easy, but there was never a lack of support, and any difficulties were quickly overcome. Important in holding all the relationships together was Bishop Njojo, who insisted that I remain a member of the Boga Diocesan and Provincial teams so that he and the church could identify with, and be identified by, what was happening in the Christian healing ministry.

Through such an approach each village selected their health priorities, while IPASC staff and students offered their technical support.

## IPASC's priority for listening to communities

A challenge for IPASC was the extent to which the Institute could be a vehicle for teaching Liverpool courses in Africa. One of IPASC's essential characteristics was the ability of staff and students to listen to and work with communities, while Liverpool's lectures confined students to classroom, laboratory and library activities.

The story of Alezo is an example of the difference between the two. Alezo was a toddler who, according to his mother, Mbusei, had died because he had lost his peace.[19] I knew that he had died of kwashiorkor, a protein-calorie malnutrition, typical in children who are followed closely by a sibling, despite the love and care that Mbusei had given. Her diagnosis was correct, in that Alezo, like so many children with kwashiorkor, looked anxious and sad, as his new-born brother had robbed him of his place at his mother's breast and on her back. Had we recognised this earlier, we, and Mbusei, could have saved Alezo's life. But our diagnosis was medical and did not make sense to Alezo's family. Had we listened to and shared with Mbusei earlier, we might have been able to save his life by restoring his peace.

IPASC could take advantage of Liverpool's teaching resources in ways in which the culture could speak through the technical information. Time spent by students in the community, and the response from local authorities, was very positive and ensured ideal working relationships.

## Back to Boga

My visits to African countries on behalf of CMC were now coloured with an awareness of strengths, weaknesses, challenges and opportunities which needed to be included in the training plans which were beginning to take shape in my mind. In early December 1991, having finished a month of lecturing in Liverpool, and having completed my contract with CMC, I was about to have some holiday.

However, on the first day of my holiday, when I turned on the radio, the headline news was that Congo was in chaos. Mobutu had refused to step down at the end of his mandate and a general strike in Kinshasa had paralysed much of the country. The exchange rate was rocketing, though money meant little to village folk for whom cash was out of reach. I was anxious to return to Congo and work with colleagues on the development of the IPASC programme.

My colleagues at Liverpool did not approve – but how could one explain? CMS did not hesitate in agreeing with my plans. Amazingly, within three working days I had a new passport, a Congolese visa, and a return ticket – and came to my senses somewhere over Italy, upstairs on a BA jumbo jet, watching Mickey Mouse. Meanwhile, CMS informed the Foreign Office, who promised to let the Ambassador in Kinshasa know of my whereabouts, in view of the emergency situation. At least the BA menu and entertainment programme had changed – blueberry gateau being a definite improvement on the walnut one of

November, and *Fantasia* a great film – but I could not keep my eyes open long enough to watch!

Shopping for cotton dresses for Rehema and Neema in England in December had been useless, so I bought some things in Nairobi. A Tearfund colleague added to my luggage with biscuits, motor-bike spare parts, and letters for Boga. When the MAF flight from Nairobi to Bunia landed, immigration formalities went well, and all seemed remarkably quiet for a country 'in chaos'. The official who waves 'table-tennis bats' around to show the pilot where to stop, embraced me, and thanked me for coming back. Customs caused no major problems, other than the usual request for anything that looked interesting in the luggage ('just a little gift?'). Most of the officials I knew well, and it was good to see them again. 'Aren't you scared to come to Congo?' they asked. When I asked if I should be, they said, 'No, but most of the other foreigners have left.'

Twenty minutes further on, at Boga, nursing staff and clergy lined the air-strip to welcome us and then filled the cathedral for the usual short service of thanksgiving for a safe arrival. A cup of coffee with the two CMS mission partners (Dr Nigel Pearson and Philip Bingham, who had remained at Boga), assured me that they were fine. I had brought Christmas goodies with me, but had forgotten to buy some bacon in Nairobi (routine shopping for anyone visiting Boga!). At home, at Nyakabale, a small village a mile from the main commercial and civic village of Boga, Amoti Kabarole and the family were waiting for me with my favourite meal (sweet potatoes and peanut sauce) on the table. Later in the day I returned to Boga to meet with Bishop Njojo and to discuss with him the idea of IPASC and its location. Since my arrival at Boga in 1982, we had worked well together, and I trusted and respected him. Now he was delighted to be part of the 'dream' and promised his support.

Chief Kisembo was amongst those waiting for me back at Amoti's house. He was eager to talk about development issues within the Collectivity of Boga.[20] He faced challenges all the way. Fuel for transport was an exorbitant price, and few people had money for 'extras'. Villagers had been working hard with him to improve their own situation: the building of bridges and killing of some of the monkeys who had been raiding the precious crops.

That evening, as most evenings at Nyakabale, I sat with the family around the dying fire of the kitchen-hut, listening once again to Neema's stories, hearing the village gossip, sharing news of England, and just enjoying the peace and simplicity of village life.

The following day, I went up to the Collectivity offices to greet the Elders, as well as the Commandant and soldiers. The Chief was enthusiastic in his welcome, and it was clearly important to him that I had returned when there was a war brewing. The Elders were quick to tell me that '*Obusinge*' still existed in Boga, and that villagers were continuing to strive for greater peace. Sitting in the Elders' hut, as I had done so often in the past, gave me a special feeling of being one with the folk of Boga and all those who had been striving against so many odds. Nevertheless, it was always a struggle to divide my time between folk who came to visit me, and having time with the children who wanted to share what they had been doing at school. They were all doing well – except Neema. For a long time we had been worried that she was severely dyslexic – an unknown term at Boga where she would never get the educational support that she needed, nor would she anywhere else in Zaïre.

As I reflected on the future, and the establishment of IPASC at Nyankunde, I knew I was going to miss life at Boga. I was at home in the community, and particularly with the Kabarole family. Sharing the local Hema and Ngety cultures had enabled me to understand so much more about health and people's expectations of health care, whether from traditional or modern health services. I was frequently travelling, but home was always there, and it was in that family home, with Amoti as matriarch, the twins as wonderful sisters, and Neema and Rehema and the other family children always being ready with stories, that I learned about the riches of African culture, and the joys of living in a Christian African family.

## Boga – Nyankunde

From Boga I went on to Nyankunde to pursue the 'Liverpool in Africa' dream with Jo and Lyn Lusi, with whom I shared a home, and with other colleagues. Jo had been in Kinshasa working on the registration of CME and IPASC with the Ministry of Higher Education. The city was apparently empty, and the shops had been ransacked. Factories were no longer functioning, and no international flights were coming into the airport which had been shot-up by excited guards – or rebels, probably on Mobutu's orders. The situation throughout the country left the health and education sectors in a precarious position, with disastrous effects on those not able to afford health care, and with malnutrition among children increasing. Because much of the infrastructure of the country had gone, many of the killer diseases, previously controlled by adequate immunisation coverage, were returning.

The situation, in which everyone in Congo was a law unto themselves, meant that usual bureaucracy had evaporated, leaving people like Jo, as Nyankunde's Medical Director (and knowing the ropes), able to legalise the two independent university colleges of CME (later to be known as ISTM/CME) and IPASC. These two institutions would be adjacent to one another, and collaborating closely, yet independent of one another. The Government encouraged us to start the courses as soon as possible, so Lyn helped me in the preparation of IPASC's courses and administration so that within a few weeks we had completed the documentation of seven three-month courses which would take us through the next three years.

An IPASC Board of Governors was formed, consisting of senior CME staff and leaders of other church-related programmes who had an interest and involvement in community health. It was at the first Board meeting, in December 1991, that some of the implications of Jo's work on IPASC's behalf became clear. I was appointed Dean of the embryonic IPASC, and Professor and head of CME's department of community health (though this was a provisional step as CME needed to get their programme off the ground). I felt dizzy with all that had happened and was not sure that I was ready for such big steps. Nor was I sure that Liverpool, upon whom we depended for the academic support, would be ready. To launch IPASC demanded a great step of faith, but did I have that amount of faith? As yet, IPASC had no staff, no buildings, furniture or equipment, and no money to back this dream. And the first course was just six months away!

## IPASC at Nyankunde

### The opening of IPASC

IPASC was born at Nyankunde on 1 June 1992, with three full-time staff members, fifteen part-time lecturers from Nyankunde Hospital, and 22 students from six African countries – and very little else. The date for the opening took advantage of the installation of Bishop Njojo as the first Archbishop of the new Anglican Province of Zaïre (30 May 1992 – St Apolo's Day).[21] We were, therefore, able to invite the international, national and local leaders who had a concern for the new Anglican Province as well as for IPASC.

IPASC's hosts, the staff of CME Nyankunde, had worked hard for the opening ceremony. Palm tree branches were decorated with flowers, and the twenty-strong hospital band lauded the occasion. Dignitaries arrived, speeches were made and IPASC was opened by the Sub-Regional Officer, to the accompaniment of the band's rendering of the Hallelujah Chorus. The emotion of that moment was intense, as I felt the months of preparing for the day melt into utter rejoicing. My eyes focused on the group of new friends and colleagues who had become the Vice Presidents and Board of IPASC, with Archbishop Njojo as the President. They had given of themselves with enthusiasm, and seemed to have adjusted to the very different approach that IPASC would be taking in its training.

I relied heavily on CMC/WCC's workshop material in preparing the whole staff for the first course. Key to this was a game called 'the Secret Box', through which a player tried to identify objects in a closed box by the sound when the box was shaken. A second player was allowed to remove the lid of the box, and to look at but not touch the objects, making a more accurate description of them. The third player, who was able to handle, smell and taste the items, should have been able to give a precise description of them but may have identified a pen as being 'red' because it had a red cap, whereas writing with it may have shown that it had blue ink. A torch may or may not be useful to give light to a community, but did the player test it to see if it worked? If it was not working, was it the battery or the bulb that needed changing? The Secret Box had an important role in IPASC's training, enabling students to recognise the characteristics, skills and challenges of a community. Students found it hard to take the Secret Box and other games as seriously as books, until they were able to use them in the community. It was then that the games were seen as convincingly powerful teaching tools.

Working with village communities helped the staff and students to understand how, in the pre-colonial era, the clan[22] was a self-sufficient micro-culture which had evolved and which dictated a way of living consistent with the preservation of the clan. This was health – not confined to the state of well-being of the individual, but relating to harmony and responsibility within the clan and the wider community. It was within the clan that most states of disharmony (physical, social or psychological) were caused and were dealt with. Each clan would have a 'specialist' who was entrusted with preventing and healing any breakdown in clan harmony, be it personal or communal, including problems as diverse as the failure of crops, drought, demon possession, sterility, measles or 'misfortune'. As family groupings have moved from extended to nuclear families, traditional health care support has weakened, and professional health care has become acceptable. Nevertheless, traditional healers criticise the superior attitude of professional staff while patients miss the familiarity of traditional practices.

In Boga, several years previous to the establishment of IPASC, the research team had spent time learning about illness (as understood locally), traditional health practices, and the decision processes related to health care in the context of the everyday life of the community. Illness ('ugonjwa') was only one of many reasons why a person may not have had health ('obusinge') and health itself was always understood as a collective word, in that it included the harmony of social relationships. Reasons for ill-health included bereavement, the loss of or damage to property and misfortune. Health care involved looking for the cause of the illness as much as giving the appropriate treatment, with the concepts of health, illness and health care being seen in relation to one another.

In the early days of transferring the model to Nyankunde, we found that communities in which students were working were keen to be involved with the new approach to training. They were delighted to be listened to and to discover their own skills. To be involved in finding answers to their own health problems was a challenge, but, on the whole, a welcome one. IPASC was establishing excellent relationships with the Chief and Elders of the community, as well as with community members and staff running health centres in the area.

A habit which began in the early days and continues today – sixteen years later – is the weekly meeting when the whole staff (then only three of us), met together to share ideas and opinions, the contribution of each being as important as that of colleagues. Kasereka, a boy of eighteen, who had applied for 'any job', was nicknamed 'Kaserol' (casserole) because he could produce something good from all that was thrown in his direction. It was at the staff meetings that Kaserol would make comments on valuable pieces of information he had picked up during the week. For example, in response to a call from a health centre, fifteen miles from Boga, Kaserol took a midwife out on the back of the motorbike to assist a woman whose life was at risk. IPASC's role in this sort of situation was not only to have a safe outcome for the mother and child, but to look into why complications had occurred and how they could be prevented in the future. For the midwife there were questions to be asked of the family and checks on the previous care given to the mother. Kaserol, dressed in the overalls he used for driving the motorbike, used his time to attend to some adjustments needed on the bike. Without paying obvious attention, he overheard the women of the family chatting . . . 'If her husband had not been drinking, he would have had the money for the care she needed, and now he will have to pay more for calling out the midwife.' 'No, it's not a drink problem . . . all the men drink the local cassava beer which we make ourselves. Our problem is that the men don't want to spend money on us. When one of us dies, they just say that it was the "Will of God". We have already lost five mothers in the village in the past month.' 'Ssh! Here comes the midwife, and she'd be angry to know what was really going on here.'

At the staff meeting the following week, Kaserol was able to share what he had learned. The response of the team was to offer to work with the villagers, training a traditional midwife (usually an illiterate, but wise woman, able to learn basic midwifery skills) who could work with the women of the village in various aspects of maternity and health care. Within three months, the villagers had a small health hut, and were visited regularly by the health team. This was the outcome of staff meetings at which everyone had a part to play and teamwork of shared thinking and planning. What was critical to these meetings and relationships with the community was the focus on listening, not just to what was being said, but also to what marginalised groups found it difficult to express.

The courses at IPASC evolved as the staff gained experience. Because the training was a new initiative in Africa, we needed to consider carefully the needs of the students as well as their employers and the communities they would be serving. Community health, if it had been defined within a health programme, often needed to be accommodated within health centres, where, for income-generating purposes, most of the emphasis would be on curative services. Community health itself, and associated preventative health-care activities, were not lucrative and the potential for community health-trained staff to make an income needed careful planning. Innovative, yet highly relevant subjects such as local herbal medicine, primary veterinary care, agriculture, water protection, conflict resolution, disaster preparedness and refugee health were, therefore, added to the full range of community health subjects.

Another important observation was that the Liverpool model did not completely satisfy either students or their sending programmes, because the training lacked Government accreditation. Putting the three-month courses together into a four-year diploma would enable IPASC to apply for recognition of its training. Two years later, IPASC was authorised to award a National Diploma in Community Health (the first institute to award such a diploma). IPASC's programme was then accepted as the national curriculum to which any subsequent community health institute had to conform.

Because these innovations were location-specific and culture-specific, the final evaluation of each student was done in his or her own programme, regardless of the country from which the student had come. The disadvantage was the cost of travel and of time involved, but it seemed a relatively small price to pay against the advantages of following up the students and the staff working with them, and being able to offer ongoing support to many groups with which I had had initial contact through CMC/WCC, and for whom that support was otherwise no longer available.

In addition to the courses being run by IPASC, workshops were developed at Nyankunde and further afield for groups of health professionals from health centres and hospitals, many of which grew from IPASC's close association with CMC/WCC. Seldom had rural staff had much encouragement or time with their peers or mentors away from their work situations, and so the workshops were much appreciated. Nurse tutors, from district hospitals, were steeped in traditional teaching practices from which they would have been nervous to deviate. As a consequence, students were taught to learn by repetition, and then found it difficult to apply their learning to practical situations. When the tutors were invited to explore new teaching techniques, once they had braved the first steps, they became excited – not just to have licence to change their approach but also to explore problem-based learning, taking courage to use interactive skills with their students and, in the end, to simply enjoy being together.

The scene was different in the Central African Republic where Kaswera, one of IPASC's experienced midwives, transformed the approach to health care for a group of volunteer village health workers who seldom received any encouragement, had little supervision and no further training to equip them for their work in isolated villages! Probably for the first time in their lives, these women lived with a well-qualified person who was passionate about her work, inspired others and never let anything pass without each person hearing a personal 'Thank you' – often for the first time in their work-related situation. Kaswera then tried to discover why there were so many deaths in the area, during or after childbirth. Based on the information the health workers were able to give her, she was able to alert them to the risks of childbirth in their community. Kaswera's approach to research helped her, and the IPASC team, to understand the pressures under which untrained, isolated rural midwives were working. This experience, building on work in which I had already been engaged in Afghanistan, led to IPASC's working on a training for illiterate traditional midwives, which became a speciality at IPASC and won WHO's approval and support.

Towards the end of 1995, we had the joy of welcoming Dr François Mwema and his family to IPASC. They had spent several years in Liverpool where François had done a Masters degree in tropical paediatrics and where the children had picked up Scouse accents! I had taught on the course, and was naturally interested in having a Christian Zairean among my students, and wondered what his plans were for the future. Could he be attracted by an invitation to return to Zaïre, or had many other more attractive proposals been offered? I also had to consider how we would ever find a budget that would make the proposal viable. Within days, another of God's plans was falling into place and with amazing support from the British immigration authorities. It was appreciated that we needed time to prepare housing for the family which would go beyond the expiration date of the family's visas. Within six months they were on their way back to Zaïre – a foreign country to the children, and definitely 'bush' to François and Pitchu. François was to head up the research and epidemiology side of IPASC's work and lost no time responding to a meningitis epidemic around Nyankunde. Students were taken from the classroom into the villages – not an unfamiliar move for them, but one which enabled the epidemic to be rapidly contained. François, Pitchu and the children had arrived, and IPASC was blessed by their having come to us.

No sooner had IPASC's four-year diploma course been recognised by the Government than IPASC was asked to develop a three-year degree course, suitable for the community health leaders of the future. Rather than students having to find the money for study overseas, and often having to cope with another language and culture, it was proposed that IPASC would have a university college with potential for offering training up to doctoral level. However, for the time being, we were still coping with the establishment of the Diploma Course, and knew that neither the budget nor space on the current three-year activity plan would accommodate such an enormous venture. Nevertheless, my teaching twice a year at LSTM gave me an opportunity to look at the resources at Liverpool to put content to what could become a Bachelor's degree in Community Health, with four sections, including: The Management of Primary Health Care; Community-Based Rehabilitation; Teaching of Primary Health Care; and Reproductive Health in the Community. The new course would require temporary accommodation, and this was offered by the Bunia Bible Institute. However, we were excited at being able to purchase 33 acres of attractive and well-positioned land four miles from Bunia town. We simply needed the money to build. At that stage we could not predict the inconveniences of the position of the land, with an army camp on the next-door campus, and with no public transport to enable students to move between the town and the campus during the years of instability which were to follow.

On the Nyankunde campus, 25 miles of rebel-lined rough road away, IPASC's well-established diploma course continued, though with inevitable limitations as a result of the insecurities in the area. What does it mean to live in 'rebel-held territory'? There was an 'uncertain quiet', meaning that life was fairly normal, but no one knew what would happen next. For weeks there were few activities but people became restless, counting the cost of no schooling, reduced work in the fields, limited trade, and little access to health care. This was a strain on staff and students. Getting back to normal in the 'uncertain quiet' was easier than living in constant anticipation of unknown rebel activity.

## Training courses

IPASC's reputation for seminars, workshops and extra courses had put added demands on the staff and kept us busy producing training materials. Further education and experience for staff was always a high priority in our planning and budgeting, and several colleagues were able to do the Liverpool Masters degree in Community Health. These colleagues shared in the excitement and the responsibilities of getting IPASC on its feet as far as relationships with the Government were concerned. They were also able to share with me my concern to continue some of the work and ethos of CMC/WCC, and so share in preparing a meeting of national heads of church-related health programmes in French-speaking Africa held at IPASC.

As we started to invest in our own resources, we were tremendously grateful for the gifts in cash and in kind. St Elizabeth's Parish, Eastbourne, took the initiative to apply to Chichester Diocese for a vehicle for IPASC. We had considered a vehicle way out of our reach, but we certainly needed one. With a trader as a friend, St Elizabeth's gift became a reality within a few weeks. It was a green Toyota Stout, able to carry twenty passengers, provided they were not looking for comfort – but no one looks for comfort on the roads or in the vehicles of Zaïre. The Toyota, purchased in 1993, made all the difference to life at Nyankunde. Sixteen years later, in a country where the life-expectancy of any vehicle is no more than four years, the IPASC Green Toyota was still the 'flag-ship' of the Institute, but more about that and her story, later.

The vehicle came at a time when we were beginning to feel the pinch of working with slender resources, and remaining heavily dependent on CME for staff and for living and teaching accommodation. In return, however, IPASC was able to help with the organisation and management of the Nyankunde Health District, though, sadly, as senior staff changes were made at CME, IPASC's role in the District diminished. With help from Tearfund, we had been able to purchase some land almost a mile from Nyankunde Hospital, beyond the airstrip. This land was added to by a gift from the community, as an expression of their gratitude that we had decided to settle among them! So as not to waste the land, we planted trees around its perimeter, and some crops, such as maize, cassava, peanuts and beans. We also started a small farm with two cows (both in calf), three rabbits and 160 chicks. The purpose of all this was to produce vegetables, milk, meat and eggs for students and to sell the surplus, as a means of reducing our costs, and having some income for extra needs. Once we took up residence on the campus, we realised that keeping animals was not as easy as reading about running livestock programmes, when one is responsible for paying salaries! We had our minds set on building a dormitory and a classroom block as well as two staff houses, and with the vehicle we were able to carry bricks and stones, enabling the builders to make good progress. However, putting up buildings suggested to authorities that there was money around. In a country that has no banks and few places in which to keep cash safely, the 'taxman' and other authorities made demands which we were not able to meet. Few of these officials have been paid for many months or years and the only way they had of making any money was by exploiting those who appear to have money (such as ourselves). In one day, five 'officials' chased us for 'favours' such as a local Chief wanting to take our new vehicle to Bunia (25 miles over a very bad road), while another wanted to tax us for our new buildings (over £600), and another for a house given to us because of an injustice, by a court order. Someone else wanted to charge us £1,000 for one day's consultancy fees, and a young man claimed tax for the 35,000 bricks we had spent three months making, and were ready to fire, in order to start building my house. We were able to argue our way out of these fictitious charges, but it was always hard work and created a stormy atmosphere.

Despite the trials and tribulations of local officials, there was always a sense of progress when we were able to respond to real needs, rather than just teaching. 'Operation IPASC' was a programme designed to curtail the cholera epidemic which had hit the Nyankunde health district. Students and staff were organised to cover the whole District. Faida (our 'reporter' and also a lecturer) covered the operation on video, getting into situations where a foreign reporter would never be allowed to tread. It was encouraging to see the number of new cases and of deaths reduced dramatically once the team had got on top of the epidemic, and exciting to see how the various health centres in the District were able to improve their services and to give the right care.

Plague, Ebola virus, meningitis, typhus and other infectious diseases became features of 'Operation IPASC', with François designing teaching programmes for control programmes for staff throughout the District. Because Ebola carried such a high infection and mortality rate, a detailed programme, including the marking of buildings, vehicles, emergency village properties and methods of cremation were all described in a detailed control programme. At the same time, other campaigns such as HIV/AIDS control, and the reduction of deaths of women at the time of childbirth, were ongoing. The maternal mortality rate was alarming, and almost all the deaths were preventable.

With IPASC being involved in so many extra work programmes, we were grateful to have some help from several 'gap year' or school leavers who offered to spend time with us. David Moore from Liverpool, who took a year out before going to Medical School, became a popular member of the IPASC team as 'Mr Fix-it' for anyone who had computer problems. He also helped with the heavy secretarial work-load as we prepared to submit our university programme to the Ministry of Higher Education in Kinshasa. Graham Gordon, a Cambridge graduate, joined the team under the auspices of Tearfund for an eighteen-month administrative placement, with some teaching. Elsbeth Schmid was a Swiss doctor who had spent considerable time in Africa and had offered to help us to develop our capacity as consultants. Following an introduction to IPASC, Elsbeth was able to join François on a journey to the west of the country, towards the Angolan border area, following up some work with which I had previously been engaged on behalf of WCC's HIV programme. It was from a Christian programme in that area that we were able to select Hendrew Lusey as WCC's HIV Co-ordinator for Central Africa.

## IPASC in Côte d'Ivoire

In 1998, IPASC expanded its work to West Africa, rather than expecting West Africans to travel to Congo. The Medical Assistance Program International (MAP),[23] with its headquarters in Abidjan, offered to host IPASC at the Christian Hospital in Dabou, Côte d'Ivoire, about 30 miles from the commercial capital of Abidjan. As in Zaïre, we were able to set up three-monthly courses similar to those with which we had started in Congo, encouraging the MAP staff to use the IPASC resources as best suited the needs of West Africa. I visited Dabou several times a year, especially in the early days, and used Dabou as a West African base for the continuation of some of the ongoing CMC/WCC-related work, particularly in the development of HIV co-ordination. Eventually, however, Kinshasa proved to be a more appropriate place for the co-ordination, and Hendrew Lusey, the WCC Co-ordinator, was the sort of colleague who was able to share his work with us, and to take some of our responsibilities.

Having an IPASC base in West Africa broadened our already wide network of contacts that existed through LSTM, WCC and CMS. There were new areas of interest that touched our professional as well as socio-cultural lives. For example, Bembèrèkè Hospital, about 400 miles north of Cotonou in Bénin, had been in discussions with LSTM's Snake Venom Department. The hospital had many snake-bite victims and was collecting as much information on the area's snakes as possible. As I walked through the grounds of Bembèrèkè, I was amazed at the number of 'near misses' I had with snakes. It was over twenty years since my first lessons on walking through snake-infested areas were given to me by an elderly Aboriginal friend, who taught me how to warn snakes of my approach (and to get out of their way). Now, in an entirely different part of the world, the old man's training was proving very useful.

Having so many new areas of interest and concern added to our 'catchment area' from West Africa was stimulating and demanding. Early-morning hours of quietness were opportunities to reflect on the previous day's activities, and on the appropriateness of responses given to questions asked. Often the next step was to pack up my things and be ready for the next journey. There were usually plenty of people able to make travel arrangements for me, as I was so often the visitor or consultant, and so was spoilt for help. But I was dependent on drivers with whom I had to communicate in French (often a very broken Creole-French), and whose road-ethics were as broken as their language, neglecting every rule in the unwritten Highway Code. Nevertheless, despite many near-misses along the roads, I always arrived at airports in record time, which was in my favour as the airports were always crowded and check-in always slow.

Visiting a country for a second or subsequent time was far easier than being a new visitor. For example, just as I was about to take a taxi from Cotonou Airport in Bénin to Bethesda Hospital, eight people alighted from a car: two IPASC Congo former students, one IPASC Abidjan student, two doctors and a pastor, a midwife and the driver – all of whom I knew. How wonderful to see them as friends and to enjoy being back with them in Bénin. It was also good to see improvements made in Cotonou since my last visit some six years previously. A pedlar carrying three ceiling fans amused me. He had one on his head being rotated rather dramatically by the wind, and one on his back. The other was in his hand. I have seen computers and sewing machines on heads, but this was a new one to me! Personal health and safety had not improved, but local initiative was lacking nothing!

At Bethesda Christian Hospital, each department was crowded. The mother and child clinic, started by one of the first IPASC Congo students seven years previously, now had over 500 mothers attending each month! The work volume was incredible, and the quality of care was excellent. Seven years ago, I had worked with our student, Perpetua, on her 'project'. She had chosen to confront the issue of breast feeding. In Cotonou, mothers were in the habit of bottle feeding their infants, following the very wrong teaching of Nestlé's posters advertising healthy looking, bottle-fed babies. Perpetua was prepared to confront the ethical, professional and socio-economic issues presented by such teaching. Now I could not avoid a sense of pride as our student told me of the talks she had been giving on national and local radio and as she showed me the posters she had designed and which the national TV company had picked up for their own publicity. And there, in the post-natal clinic area of Bethesda Christian Hospital, was a crowd of very content and very healthy mums and babies.

That day, lunch was shared with the staff of Bethesda at a nearby 'restaurant' – where we had a local dish of cassava, maize meal, fish and pork with a slimy green leaf and peanut sauce eaten with our fingers. After lunch we went to Yesuku ('Jesus' home'). Twenty years ago, part of a Muslim tribe had become Christians: they had been persecuted, so left their village-on-stilts in a lagoon and moved to the coast of the mainland. Later they found a sheltered cove on the coast, and built their homes on stilts again. To reach the village we needed to wade out to a pirogue and then we were 'punted' through the waters until we reached the end of the village. A former IPASC student had spent the past seven years working with the community and now the villagers had just built a small health centre (on stilts) in split bamboo. When we arrived they were painting it – in sky blue and psychedelic pink!

We were given (another) meal, after meeting with the health committee. The previous day we had five meals – could we get away with only four today? But the hard work was always compensated with entertainment of children, and here we had primary schoolchildren managing their pirogues. One of the Bethesda team asked if there was a little salt available for the meal. 'Yes' came the quick reply, and a tiny tot was dispatched 'next door' to get some salt – but 'next door' was a pirogue ride away. The child deftly untied the pirogue, jumped in and darted off, zigzagging between men with fishing nets and women (in their pirogues) selling their wares and fruit. He was back before we had finished chuckling at the bizarre but delightful situation! Back to work, the last stop of the day was the evaluation of a recent IPASC Abidjan student. She was teaching a small class of health promoters, and her students had to put on a play about nutrition before her lesson got under way.

The next morning, once we were through the usual traffic jam, we went to a mother and child health clinic, the results of which were very exciting. At least 80% of the infants in the 40,000 population for which the hospital is responsible, are fully immunised. Seven years ago there was an immunisation coverage of 5%! For me to see a former IPASC student make such exceptional progress was very special. An interesting initiative she had used to reach mothers in the poorest slums was the establishment of 'street clinic'. Every day the team was out on the streets, usually under a tree on a street corner, seeing and immunising mothers and children. It was a very good way to serve those who would otherwise be unable to get to the clinic because they did not have the right clothes to put on (people do not like wearing rags in public places).

Lomé, the capital of Togo, was only two hours further along the palm-lined coastal Bénin–Togo border road. Immigration formalities were simple, and a professor from the medical school in Lomé was waiting for me at the border, and took me to his home just another hour away. As a visitor I am usually shy and nervous of doing the wrong thing. Staying with people from a culture which I did not know was worse. However, the family made me welcome. No sooner had we arrived than my hosts asked me to join them for a church meeting. I had no idea what it was all about, but followed like a lamb. Then I discovered that the professor had been asked to address a women's group about family planning and HIV/AIDS. He asked me to share with the women, although I found myself in an almost impossible situation. I could not understand the local Creole language, which the women preferred, and, because we were late arriving, did not know what had already been said nor what had been omitted; but I was expected to jump straight in, in French, with translation. Neither subject can be touched without understanding the culture. I did not even know what sort of church I was in! Whatever I said must have been acceptable, and the rest of the evening passed without incident – though I was still trying to figure out what type of church we had attended. The professor showed me their translation of the Bible, which looked the same as most old Bibles, while his wife tied a coloured scarf on my head suggesting that I might have been in a closed Brethren church.

## Partners with IPASC in West Africa

Although we had a willing English partner in Edouard Yao and the Medical Assistance Programme of which Edouard was the West African Regional Director, IPASC of West Africa (IPASC WA) was more a consortium of partnerships. It was important for us to establish relationships, and so, for example, on a coconut plantation Edouard took the top off a coconut for me and I drank the delicious milk – which I shared with the local Chief, just back from fishing in the lagoon. Together we discussed with the Chief the vision of his people to work with IPASC in improving the health of communities.

Conferences were good places for making new partners. I was speaking at one such conference for church-related health programmes in Jos, Northern Nigeria. During the tea and coffee breaks I took advantage of getting to know the participants, and the situations in which they were working. Most of them were from European backgrounds which were very different from the type of person I had met until then. Some had been students at LSTM, and so it was useful to see to what extent they had benefited from their Liverpool studies, and to what extent, either at Liverpool or at IPASC, we should be improving the content of the courses. It was interesting for me to see the extent to which primary health care and staff management were issues of concern that kept arising, not as having had insufficient training but rather of a sense of inadequacy in running primary health-care programmes. Usually, those who wanted more help were those from religious communities or church-related backgrounds, who were looking for help which was seldom available in their work area. It pointed to the importance of CMC/WCC.

Just over the Nigerian border was the Life Abundant Programme in Banso (LAP), Cameroun, from the Baptist Community Health Programme (from the English-speaking side of Cameroun). My visit to Banso introduced me to a partnership with LAP whereby we would be able to respond, in a small way, to the needs of English-speaking church-related health programmes in Africa.

On the horizon was, first, a week in Kenya on a World Health Organisation consultative board discussing 'Poverty and Health' (though discussions would never solve the problems). From Kenya my colleague, Sabuni, and I would go to Zimbabwe for the seven-yearly Assembly of the World Council of Churches, where we have been invited to present the ministry of IPASC.

Let me leave you with a thought from Abidjan. A professor of anthropology introduced me to the 'dja' of the Akan tribe. The 'dja' is a packet made of skin or leaves, containing miniature representations of concepts, values and traditions of the Akan culture. The 'dja' is opened annually for the instruction of the young people concerning their ancient culture. Another important symbol is a bird perched on a pyramid looking back over its tail. This symbolises that before making decisions about change, we should look back to our 'dja' and compare new ways with old, and then only make changes if the new is better than the old. What would be in your 'dja'? When we know what the hidden contents of the 'dja' are, we can begin to consider how best to respond to (health) needs in a culturally acceptable way, and through a Christian (healing) ministry.

## Editors' note

*From this point on, you will be reading extracts from Pat's CMS Link Letters (LL) and other notes which she had assembled as resources for her book. These are the unthreaded beads; some might yet have been discarded, others trimmed for size or further polished, but all may be valued in themselves.*

### LL71: May 1995

*Another very heavy cloud: we have just heard of the sudden death in England of Nyakato Kabarole, twin sister of Nyangoma. Nyakato, who was studying in Whitby, had a cerebral haemorrhage and died in hospital, in Hull. Her body is being flown home next week (thanks to the understanding of Tearfund, her sponsors). She will be buried next to the cathedral, so that history will record the important leadership role of women in the diocese during this decade. Some of you will know that the twins and I have always shared a home – whether in Boga, Nyankunde or in England. I will miss a very dear friend and sister.*

### LL72: 2 August 1995

*As I prepare to return to Zaïre (on 6 August) I thought you might like an update on Nyangoma's health following Nyakato's death from a congenital kidney condition. Nyangoma was found to have the same underlying kidney disease as her sister but we are delighted there is no aneurysm. She will need treatment for the kidney disease for the rest of her life – but can return to continue an otherwise normal lifestyle.*

### LL73: November 1995

*Three of us went to the local parish church – a mud church with a leaky thatch roof where some people had brought stools to sit on, the rest sat on logs left in the church. I was given a chair from the 'vicarage' (another mud hut). The service was special because it brought to a conclusion a seminar on AIDS in the parish. Some Christians from Uganda had come over to help the vicar – they all had AIDS and wanted to help youngsters and couples to change their lifestyles, so that they would not have sorrow and suffering in their families. Sadly, for many it is too late. The incidence of AIDS at Nyankunde is steadily increasing, and the age of attack is decreasing as older men look for younger girls. While AIDS is an enormous problem, there are still many other health hazards all around.*

*Three of our staff have been out in the bush this week trying to hunt down a source of meningitis about 60 miles from here. They put the motorbike in one of the small planes and flew to the nearest air-strip. We lost touch with them for a few days, until they returned – almost unrecognisable! They were bruised and filthy, tired but happy! They had tracked through the forest, visited health centres and village homes. Finally they discovered the epicentre of the epidemic (as well as discovering many other major health problems). Now we have to do something about it, hopefully with some expert help from our colleagues at the Liverpool School of Tropical Medicine.*

*Discovering the root causes of diseases is very much on our agenda, but it is not useful if we are not able to do anything about them. The major barrier to caring and curing people is the poverty all around us. In a country where full costs of medical care are borne by the patient or the family, few people can afford adequate treatment. For this reason, we arranged a seminar for our staff and students on herbal medicines. We discovered that within 500 metres of our classroom there were at least 25 medicinal plants – that cost nothing. The students were enthusiastic as they used these plants to make simple medicines, as well as discovering how to introduce some appropriate technology into powder and creams. Did you know that baby powder could be made from cassava flour? Or that skin cream can be made from candles and kitchen oil, with a couple of handfuls of lemongrass (which grows everywhere) to give it a good perfume? Add some local pepper (pili-pili) and you have a cream for rheumatism, or neem leaves to ensure that mosquitos keep their distance. In working with communities we need to ensure that health care is practical and affordable, or we are wasting our time. How much money do we waste in Europe on expensive medicines or exotic creams?*

*Since I have been back in Zaïre, I have been travelling considerably (as usual). Immediately on my return in August, I went to Tanzania to work with a programme at Kilimatinde which has received considerable support from Tearfund. After one week back here, Kaswera and I went to Kuluva Hospital in Arua, Uganda, to lead the first IPASC course conducted in English (again, with the collaboration of*

*Tearfund). This went very well, apart from a security alert in the West
Nile area of Uganda, which made us feel as though we were at home
(security alerts are very familiar to us in Zaïre). After a couple of weeks
back here, Kaswera went to Malawi to represent IPASC at a consultation and I went to Zimbabwe to join colleagues from Geneva (World
Council of Churches and the International Red Cross IFRCRCS) to
reflect on how we can better enable communities to reach a reasonable
standard of health. Kaswera and I are on the move again next week,
when Kaswera goes to a consultation on scholarship funding in
Nairobi, and I go to Manila (Philippines) to present a paper on
training health professionals at community level. I will be representing
our own Institute as well as the World Council of Churches.*

*Meanwhile, the new academic year has got off to a good start with
nineteen students from Zaïre, Burundi, Angola, Bénin and Guinea.
Tomorrow brings a special treat for us with the arrival of Sally Shand
and Brenda Cook from St Mary's Church in Upton (Wirral). Sally
is our Commissary in England, and Brenda the Mission Secretary.
We really look forward to seeing them before they go to Boga to visit
Nyangoma.*

### February 1996

*Lecturing in Liverpool for a month twice a year is refreshing and stim-
ulating. I lecture in English (marvellous to write handouts in an hour
instead of a week!), and, at the end of the day, I go home to relax (or
to prepare the next day's lectures), with no fear of students or staff
attacking me with impossible demands!*

*More contracts are looming ahead. I have seen much of Africa, but
there are some countries which I have never visited, and which have
cultures very different from most of sub-Saharan Africa. In May I will
be going to Madagascar and Ethiopia, and hope to learn something of
the cultures of those areas.*

*One thing that has not changed much over the last year or so has
been the Rwandan refugee situation in Goma. Now, with threats from
the Zairean Government that camps will close, we wonder about the
repercussions for Zaïre, as well as for the refugee community. The situation in Burundi is threatening to explode, and we can only pray that
it will be contained, and that Bujumbura and other areas will confront
the issues of human rights and not fall to the same fate as Rwanda did*

*in 1994. IPASC remains in touch with activities in the camps, and over the border in Rwanda.*

### LL75: October 1996

*The link between Liverpool and IPASC is growing stronger as we become better established. During my teaching spell at Liverpool in September, two colleagues (both of whom had taught at IPASC) and I presented a seminar which increased the interest among those who were not aware of the breadth of our activities. In the near future we are likely to have more collaborative research, and more visits from Liverpool staff. The present group of Liverpool students includes several CMS Mission Partners, and the medical director of a hospital in Bénin, whose colleagues are studying at IPASC at present. It is interesting to be teaching the boss in Liverpool and his immediate junior at IPASC!*

*During the school holidays I had Neema and Rehema, our two girls from Boga, together with their friend Mugisa, to stay. The day after they arrived another little friend, Simon, arrived from Bukaringi, announcing that he had also come to stay (he had walked 40km across the hills to reach Nyankunde). I began to panic! What was I to do with four children, while the accounts, annual report and project proposals were all competing for time? 'Mama, your peanuts are ready for harvest, and you have left your sweet potatoes in the ground too long – we'll see to them tomorrow.' So my concern changed to joy and I loved having the children. They seemed to have grown up so quickly and are now very capable of looking after themselves – and looking after me (even to the point of breakfast in bed at 5.30am!).*

### LL77: February 1997

*While I was in Nairobi I took the opportunity of visiting three colleagues from IPASC, all of whom are studying there. I had a very happy day with Elias, studying Business Management at the Nazarene University, and another day with Faida, doing a Master's degree in Communications, and Alege doing a Bachelor's degree in Development Studies – both at Daystar University. Meanwhile, Paluku Sabuni completed his Master's degree in Community Health at Liverpool (1995), and has gone to Nairobi to be with others waiting for an opportunity to return to Zaïre (where his family lives). As previously planned, I spent three weeks in South Africa, during January (1997). I was with Dr Remy Toko and family (formerly my neighbours at Nyankunde, until they left last year [1996] for Remy to train in Paediatrics). Their home is in Johannesburg, and from there I visited one of our advisers – Det Prozesky, an external evaluator in Pretoria, to discuss IPASC's future. I then went to Cape Town, and met up with Sally Shand (from home) for a very happy week's holiday in Knysna (over 400km east of Cape Town) where the sea was warm and the scenery beautiful. Back in Cape Town I attended an important conference, where I made many new friends and met old ones (some from as far back as my Bangladesh days of 1975–79).*

*Now back in England, I have two weeks teaching at Liverpool before packing my bags again and returning to Uganda for a couple of days. At the end of February I will have a week or so at the University of the Suez Canal in Ismailiya, Egypt (where I will be filling in for one of my Zairean colleagues). I am not sure where I will be based after Ismailiya – probably in Nairobi, but, wherever I am, our old address should always find us (after a time!).*

### LL79: 13 July 1997

*Some friends of ours were prepared to face the challenges of the future. A few weeks ago Vejay, an Asian friend, who is a trader, came to visit us. He told us of his entrepreneurial plans for the future – trade which would serve the population. It was noon, and we urged him to stay for a meal. He refused, saying that he had to catch a plane that afternoon from Bunia. A few hours later, just 12km from us, Vejay's plane crashed, exploding as it hit the ground. Between us we knew most of the 27 people aboard, including the Israeli pilot. It was chaotic here as we made makeshift accommodation for relatives who came to the hospital to try to identify the bodies of the passengers. The charred remains were ghastly to look at, but, compared to the agony of the camps and the destitution of Marabo, somehow one could reconcile the disaster as being 'a tragic accident'. That is easier to cope with than deliberate genocide or sheer destitution.*

## LL80: *January 1998*

*I have just arrived back in the Democratic Republic of Congo (or DRC as the old Zaïre has become known) from a trip to Rwanda, where I have been looking at a water programme, in preparation for a workshop I will be leading there in January. A weekend at home is always a treat as I have been away so much lately, and it is good to be able to catch up with some administration. I am always behind with accounts, correspondence and report writing, but the Christmas holiday promises some space to deal with these.*

*Being in Rwanda after DRC, one is impressed by the level of development. The main roads are superb, there are telephones, more or less constant electricity and water (in the towns), and public transport. Government structures are in place and functioning – though lacking resources – and people generally seem enthusiastic about development. We long for the day when we will have that level of utilities and communications in DRC. However, under the relative development in Rwanda, the country and the people are still hurting from very deep emotional and physical wounds. Being there was a very sobering experience. I met a war widow who was caring for nineteen children (mostly orphans of her brothers) and had no work. Another woman was still in shock, her husband having been among the hundreds slaughtered in the Mundende camp last week (while I was there). In one village I visited, two-thirds of the homes were headed by widows, while many others were headed by teenagers who had lost their parents. One of the many 'war-widows' clubs in Kigali had a membership of over 3,000. This situation is typical of most areas. One health worker quietly expressed her confusion: 'We're animals. How could we ever allow the genocide to happen?'*

*The Archbishop of Rwanda is Kolini, the former Bishop of Shaba in DRC. He was invited to be Bishop of Kigali only a few months ago and shortly afterwards was elected Archbishop. He is trying to come to terms with the implications of being Archbishop in a new country and in such exceptionally difficult circumstances. He told me that hundreds of the priests had been killed during the genocide, while others had not come back to their parishes. Pastoral work was virtually abandoned during the war and now there is much to catch up on. Last week the Archbishop confirmed 460 people – in one parish! The training of clergy and church leaders is high on his agenda but he insists that he is not prepared to ordain anyone who does not have a Christian message with which to challenge and comfort the hurting people of Rwanda. I came away from Rwanda feeling that we were in no position to judge or even to understand. Our response can only be to hold our brothers and sisters in prayer and allow the Holy Spirit to heal and recreate. The same is true for those in Burundi. Unfortunately, I had to cancel my planned visit there because of insecurity on the roads. Back in Congo, with few of the utilities or communications enjoyed in Rwanda, life is tense. While I was in Goma, on my way back from Rwanda, there was a long period of shooting, while today, back at Nyankunde, I learned that a couple of days ago a driver had been shot and three of our doctors attacked not far from here. There have been other incidents which remind us that we are still going through a very difficult and insecure period. However, in some areas there are changes. We have to remember that the new Government is coping with a huge country (in comparison, Rwanda is tiny), and has inherited the bankruptcy and bad habits of the former Government.*

*Like much of eastern Africa, we have had prolonged heavy rains, and roads (mud tracks) are now virtually impassable. Even air travel is difficult as pilots often have to cancel flights or change schedules. Flying in this weather is like being in a maze-in-the-air as the pilot negotiates altitudes and directions to get around, or under, or over storms. I look anxiously at the instruments, calculating how long before we land. I enjoy flying in the small planes, but I do not enjoy aeronautics!*

*Before going to Rwanda, I was in Kisangani, our Provincial capital (700km from here), helping to facilitate a Government seminar for district medical officers dealing with the surveillance and control of epidemics. It was a good experience, and I appreciated time to get to know the doctors of the province as well as some of the new authorities. Until now, IPASC has run similar seminars for doctors, but I was very encouraged to be part of a Government team, which also used the resources of UNICEF, and the World Health Organisation. The subject itself (epidemics) is important as we continue to fight against cholera, typhoid, plague, sleeping sickness, polio, and many other infectious diseases, not to mention tuberculosis and AIDS-related diseases.*

*Recently I mentioned to you the village of Marabo which had dropped into the pit of utter poverty and despondency following the war and the drought. Some of you enquired anxiously about the folk there, while some sent gifts (used to construct a water source for the village).*

*The simple support that we have been able to share has brought amazing results. This week the village leader brought me £25 to look after for the village health centre (just built by them). The money had been collected from patients treated at the health centre (no free medical care here) and will be used for the nurse's salary.*

*Meanwhile, a group of mothers are feeding the malnourished children (over half the children between one and five years old). Many of the children are so much better that they are playing, laughing and singing again. It has been a lesson for me, as our simple love and concern, and a little support, have enabled a community to find its feet. The committee members came to thank the IPASC team for their help today, and asked me to pass on their thanks to you, for your prayers, gifts and support. I felt so humble. They had done most of the work themselves, climbing out of their pit through their own effort. Now they are looking to the future, and are making mud bricks so they can improve their hut which serves as a health centre.*

*Last week a plane arrived from Nairobi with several weeks' worth of mail. Among the many letters was a bumper-bundle of Christmas cards for me. Thank you for your greetings and your love. Many of the letters expressed concern at the theft of our motorbike. It is a long story, but Mamie, our Administrator, found it at Bunia airport, just as it was being loaded into a plane for Kisangani! What a miracle, and what a relief! We had to pay quite a lot to the various authorities to get it back, but not nearly as much as we would have paid for a new motorbike! Here the story is still being told, because it is so rare to retrieve stolen goods!*

*This Christmas the people of Nyankunde have been remembering the war of 21–25 December 1996, when about 150 houses were burned and a number of people killed. Our friend Diabo, cruelly dragged from his house and shot, would have been happy this weekend to see his first son (educated by IPASC) marry a delightful young lady. Painful memories were mixed with thanks as folk look forward to a happier Christmas this year. In the past few days, various choirs have been rehearsing carols and the youth have been practising a play.*

### Fatuma

*Fatuma (Fatu) came to us at Nyankunde as a diploma student. She had struggled at school and we were not sure that she would be able to manage the course, though she was determined to learn how to help people in the community. Fatu had spent much of her life living with her aunt in Bunia, although her parents came from an area several hundred miles south of Bunia where there was a very different language and culture. Nevertheless, having been through secondary schooling at Bunia, Fatu had been able to adapt. She was a Roman Catholic and, through her involvement with the local Catholic Church, fitted in well with the church community.*

*Fatuma's family was far from rich and, because she was not the child of the family, she had to work hard to find money for her training fees. She had a love of clothes, and dressing correctly was important to her. Often she would ask if she could clean my house, or look after the garden so she had cash for those extras.*

*During her third year, Fatu had several bouts of 'malaria' – a diagnosis which is often used in a non-specific way. It was the head of training who noticed that the doctor treating her had done a test for HIV, but there was no indication of what part this played in her illness of 'malaria'. I asked the doctor responsible for her care, only to discover that her HIV test had proved positive, but she had not been told about the test having been done, or that she had the HIV infection. Although there were plenty of patients with HIV, this was the first known case we had had among the IPASC family. It was a devastating experience.*

*Papa Unega, the Chaplain, and myself left our doors open 24 hours of the day for Fatu. She went through all the stages of pain, bereavement and self-rejection. She was angry, hurt, and felt that God had deserted her. But she maintained her dignity and gradually began to think through her situation. Always to be childless? – No! Any hope of marriage? Yes! Could she still train as a midwife? Yes! Her questions built up a new profile for Fatu who had not expected that she could live a relatively normal life. Three of us kept her secret until she was ready to tell the staff, and then her student colleagues. There was an aura of appreciation as the staff and students admired Fatu's courage. For her practical year, Fatu chose to work with hospital patients with HIV; to design pastoral care, in collaboration with the hospital chaplain. The impact was significant as Fatu was able to relate to parents, to children, to various people in the community who, in one way or another, were living with HIV. With an ecumenical group, she visited programmes in Uganda, to learn how to work with people living with HIV. Gaining a distinction for her practical work, Fatu was committed to beginning an HIV programme at IPASC, which has been growing ever since.*

## LL82: December 1998

*The problems are compounded by heavy rains and no infrastructure to repair washed-out roads (hence the 25-mile journey from Nyankunde to Bunia now takes about six hours!). This week we have heard of serious looting of some of the Anglican property, and of other injustices. Rebel leaders are encouraging the resumption of normal activities, and even inviting mission partners to return, but church leaders do not advise this at present.*

## LL83: 20 March 1999

*About half of our students come from church-related programmes, while the rest have been sent by the Government. The religious mix (Muslim, Pagan and Christian) is reflected among the students, with only a third being Christian. In this heterogeneous group I find myself an onlooker as lecturers and some students take a typically evangelical stance. The day begins with prayers led by students and, while not obligatory, is attended by all students. The routine (hymn, prayer and talk) is rather monotonous, and the emphasis on hell, fire and damnation, with little about the love and mercy of God, seems to me to be very one-sided (my being sensitive to the position of the non-Christians present). The forcefulness with which the message is given imposes on the listener. As I observe, I wonder how we as Christians (at home or abroad) come over to our non-Christian friends. Are we lukewarm or are we so forceful and imposing to the point of arrogance that we put people off the Gospel? Or indeed is our Gospel the whole Gospel including the love and mercy of God as well as the forgiveness of sin? It has been quite a challenge to be an observer.*

*In Dabou I have been attending the local Methodist church (there is no Anglican church in Côte d'Ivoire). One needs to be at the church at least half an hour before the service to be sure to get a seat! At each service there are several choirs which sing lustily and with joy. I have never sung the Venite at such a speed (least of all in French), and accompanied by so much dancing! Maybe this is how David expected his Psalms to be sung, as it is certainly a 'joyful noise' sung unto the Lord! (Anglicans could learn a few things from this congregation, especially those in Congo!)*

*Travelling between Liverpool, Kenya, Uganda and Côte d'Ivoire, with occasional trips to Europe, make Gatwick Airport a familiar transit area (even the tax-free shopkeepers know me!). I do not mind the travel but am developing a 'restless spirit', always moving on after a few days or weeks. The diversification of interests prevents me really committing myself to any one place or interest area. Yet there are increasing demands upon IPASC and upon myself. IPASC seems to be filling a void in responding to the needs and potential of French-speaking Africa. We are becoming a resource for the translation of health materials, experts at a 'community approach' to health provision, and trainers for various levels of health professionals.*

## LL84: 24 June 1999

*During the past few months I have spent most of my time in Côte d'Ivoire, working on IPASC materials. In May we hosted a World Council of Churches pharmaceutical workshop in Abidjan, which was for Christian health programmes from French-speaking Africa and the Caribbean. Some participants were old friends whom I had met in various parts of Africa. One was a European friend who had worked in Africa for many years. Our paths had frequently crossed. The last time I visited him was during a period of intense insecurity in the country in which he lives. He had just married a local girl and they were blissfully happy. Her three children were with them. Now he is a widower, his wife having died of AIDS eighteen months ago.*

*The youngest child, the fruit of rape by a soldier, is infected. My friend is also HIV-positive. As he let me into his secret fears and the hidden turbulence of his life, he sobbed. I hung on to him as he talked at great length. Living with AIDS in Africa is something that is familiar to us. There is always pain, but usually, within the African context, fear is softened by the love and support of the extended family, and by faith in God. My friend has nothing and no one to support him . . . few friends, and certainly none with whom he can share this sort of news. He told me how the other staff members were always too busy to talk! He has no faith – despite working in a Christian team. He is a very lonely and frightened person, facing death at 35 – a European with AIDS in Africa, and caring for his African step-children alone. How often we miss the precious moments of sharing with someone in desperate need, because we are 'too busy'.*

*News from Nyangoma in Boga is somewhat distressing. The medical* team is trying to cope with two epidemics: meningitis and cholera. IPASC's Rapid Response Team cannot respond because there are no MAF planes (which were taken out of the country when the war started) and even health teams cannot move about freely. There is no emergency funding available and medicines are very difficult to get hold of. Even if medicines were available, they could not be distributed because of the rebel occupation. Sabuni will come to England, having been awarded a scholarship for his PhD studies. He will have a reading month in Liverpool before beginning some studies at Makerere University, Uganda. We thank God for the scholarship from the German Institute of Medical Missions (DIFAEM).

I will spend the next few months mainly in Abidjan, but with a trip to the USA where I will be at a WHO and UNESCO workshop in Tucson (on 'Universities and the Health of the Disadvantaged'), and then visiting the international headquarters of the Medical Assistance Programme (our partners in Abidjan), in Atlanta. I hope that my next letter may bring news of my return to Congo.

### LL85: 26 September 1999

**Thursday, 22 July:** A good flight to Abidjan (Côte d'Ivoire). Edouard Yao, our partner, was at the airport with Dr Manoj Kurian, Executive Secretary of the health desk of the World Council of Churches (WCC). We had agreed to meet in Abidjan so I could introduce Manoj to some of the work in French-speaking Africa. We have called together folk from a few of the West African countries to meet him.

**Sunday, 25 July:** I took Manoj and other visitors who had arrived from Senegal, Togo and Burkina Faso, to the Methodist church – to enjoy the taste of paradise!

**Monday–Wednesday, 26–28 July:** We began a conference on church-related health programmes with particular reference to HIV/AIDS programmes. I was acting as translator, facilitator and secretary! On the whole the conference went well.

**Tuesday, 3 August:** In the morning Theodore and Agnes drove me to the bus station. It was crowded, noisy, colourful and confusing! No one 'talked' but everyone shouted. The passengers sat on the bus waiting for the driver for fifteen minutes, during which an ' ambulant healer' tried to sell his wares. Migraine, infertility and 'flu could be treated by the same medicine – one spoon three times a day for one disease and only two spoons a day for another. There was medicine to make your teeth white and another to heal the br . . . br . . . in your stomach. So now we know! The bus coughed and spluttered its way through the city, with the coughs blending into a paroxysm as we hit the motorway. No sooner had we got up a little speed than we were stopped by the police, who inspected our identity cards.

Those who had no identity card were taken off the bus. After two hours we arrived at Dabou, where I was following up a couple of our students who are trying to maintain a community health programme in a hospital where income from curative care is the priority.

**Sunday, 8 August:** Before leaving for church the professor's wife handed me a head-scarf (apparently imperative for church – and I did not have one). During the service, when the chalice was passed around, I was left out . . . So that was it – I was in a closed Plymouth Brethren Assembly – but a very friendly one! My student arrived at 3pm as planned, with her pastor. The pastor did more talking than she did. He was looking for money to build a dispensary for the church. This did not win my sympathies as it appeared to be a typical 'project' to earn credibility for the church, but which would inevitably end in discord, misappropriation of funds, and failure. It would not even be legal and certainly would not conform to IPASC's ideals of collaborating with government health systems to assure sustainability. In Togo, medicines are very freely available – anything can be purchased without prescription – particularly from hawkers and pedlars.

**Monday, 9 August:** The professor's wife prepared a nice Togolese meal for me. I was now feeling more at home – always the way when one is leaving! However, I will be glad to be back in Abidjan and can spread out beyond my suitcase. The flight back to Abidjan was uneventful, with faithful Theodore at the airport to meet me – despite being 1am.

**Thursday, 12 August:** A journey had been arranged for me to visit seven of our Ivorian students. Theodore picked me up at 6am and we arrived at the first stop, Tiassalé, by 8am. The two students there are *working with the District Health Authority – a government pilot district (i.e. meant to be experimenting with new approaches to health care). The students had made almost no progress at all.*

*The next stop was a couple of hours further on at Lakota, where three students from a non-government organisation were working. The welcome was enthusiastic, everything was ready for me to see and a wonderful meal had been prepared. We went into the villages to meet with tribal chief and village elders, and discussed their progress. It was a truly impressive presentation.*

*The comparison between government and non-government organisations is amazing. These three young men (the administrator, the director and the doctor) had come, as a team, to IPASC. They had taken everything in, worked on a programme (including much of the material from IPASC) and made it work. They did not have much money, but their enthusiasm and initiative carried them through. We spent over five hours with them (too long), and were happy to have a little ceremony with the chiefs and village health workers, to present their diplomas.*

*Three hours later we arrived at Guiglio, near the border with Liberia. I had arranged to stay with some Irish UFM missionaries, who made me very welcome. They seldom see foreigners, so the children pounced on me with books and toys. I had brought a few chocolates and biscuits and they responded as though I had brought a huge gift! I had a wonderful hot shower (first hot shower since I left the UK!).*

***Friday, 13 August:*** *I discussed the problems of community health policy and planning with the District Medical Officer and promised to follow up some points with the Ministry of Health. Here is the third of three pilot health districts, and they do not even have a vehicle to reach their population spread over a 150km by 100km area. We have two students here who I visited. The 350-mile journey back to Abidjan took just over six hours. The scenery and the village houses are not unlike Congo – the big difference being the good roads! We stopped at Yamoussoukro – where the previous President built a Basilica (it was his home town) – second in size to St Peter's, Rome. It is beautiful and enormous but I have some problems with its appropriateness in a small town in Côte d'Ivoire! We arrived home at 6pm. I was shattered, and so grateful to find that I could have a room at the WEC Guest House.*

**Tuesday, 17 August:** *This was the day of my journey that brought me most fear and anticipation of joy – travelling to Kinshasa (DR Congo). So much could go wrong. Soldiers were in evidence from the beginning on the runway at Kinshasa airport, and I felt myself freeze (I am still allergic to Congolese soldiers!).*

*Immigration and customs were very easy (the airport has been transformed from the cattle market of pre-Kabila days!). Before I was through immigration, the protocol officer from the Protestant Council was waving at me! I felt I had come home (despite the soldiers). Dr Marini, President of the Protestant Council, was waiting for me at the guest house.*

*This evening, as I sat in Dr Marini's home, I had to keep pinching myself. Was I really in Congo, and with no problems on the way? Back at the guest house, I turned on the BBC News and heard that fighting was continuing in Kisangani between Ugandans and Rwandans (700 miles to the east). How ironic – other people's war in the middle of this country, when the nationals just want to get on with living! The Kinshasa mosquitoes were out in force to welcome the foreigner!*

**Wednesday, 18 August:** *Perhaps the highlight of the day came in the evening – a visit from Bishop Mutangalaiya with his wife and one of his pastors. As soon as they arrived, the Bishop led us in prayer, giving thanks for this wonderful reunion. Mama was in tears, and my tears were only just hidden. This little team must have one of the most important and most difficult missionary tasks, and yet they face it with confidence and courage. To live and work in Kinshasa, and in the slum areas, must be extremely difficult, and then to cover such a vast area (much larger than England) with only seven clergy and with no communications makes it virtually impossible. There is no health care at all in some areas, and the Bishop has already asked the permission of the district medical officer for a health centre.*

*This request has been warmly welcomed by the authorities, but now it is a problem of finding the money. The Bishop wants to send a student to IPASC and, of course, will be given a priority place. Imagine a bishop having no contact with his brother bishops! He is Assistant Bishop of Kisangani Diocese but there is no possibility of contact with his senior bishop there. He is hoping to travel via Nairobi to Uganda for a meeting with CMS and the other Congolese bishops – a journey costing £900 (but met by CMS) and taking several days. In England a telephone call costing a few pence would bring him in contact with anyone he needed. I felt very small beside this spiritual giant and his faithful team. Their love for me flowed liberally, but my respect for them grew enormously. They left to write letters for Boga and Bunia for me to take to Uganda tomorrow. Their old Land Rover, which is held together with various pieces of tape, cord and wire, needed some manipulation before it started. A petrol-soaked rag was held over a pipe somewhere in the bowels, and the engine mysteriously coughed into action. The entourage jumped in, putting back the door that had fallen off in the process, and doing up odd cords. They waved until we lost sight of one another – leaving me in deep thought about this irrepressible team facing more problems than we can ever imagine, and oozing with the love of Jesus.*

*My travels took me on to Kenya (to complete an evaluation) and Uganda (where I met IPASC colleagues from Congo, and spent ten days doing accounts together), and then I returned to England – having been in fifteen guest houses, twenty beds, and ten countries in eight weeks! Sabuni came to England with me (he has a scholarship for a pre-PhD month of reading).*

### LL86: 21 November 1999

*I am in Bangalore for a World Health Organisation advisory group on poverty and health, and a South East Asian Conference on the same subject. The meetings went well and gave me time to learn from the rich experiences of India.*

*In Bangalore I was able to see some of the outreach work of St John's College (a Roman Catholic medical college) which uses an innovative approach to facilitating communities to take control of their own lives in health and development issues. One of the keys to their success seems to be their insistence on using only female health workers in the villages and concentrating on women's groups for the promotion of development activities. Their theory is that women working in health will be concerned for the overall development of their community, while men are more often looking for economic satisfaction and employment potential. At the end of a day spent with some village women they asked me about the women in Africa. When I shared with them something of the situation in Congo, they stood up and said they would go to Africa and fight with the women until they had freedom and health-*

*ier lifestyles. I was very moved by this expression of solidarity, albeit an impossible proposition for the moment. Nevertheless, it planted the seeds of an idea for an India to Congo exchange for the future.*

*From Bangalore I caught a night bus to Vellore. That was quite an experience, and I was so thankful to have a travelling companion who knew the ropes! It seems that life in India never really comes to a stop, not even at night. At 2am we were still travelling bumper-to-bumper and continued to do so for most of the six-hour drive!*

*The bus was noisy, the horn screamed out regularly and the vehicle shuddered and clattered at the slightest of bumps – which were endless! But, at least there is a very effective public transport system, and a good network of roads in India. The 200km cost me only £2.50, and that was a luxury ticket (I am glad I did not go for the 60p ordinary bus!!!).*

*Coming to Vellore Christian Medical College has been something of a pilgrimage. Since first going overseas with CMS, I have longed to visit this world-renowned University College. I have had the joy of staying with two very special Indian friends, both consultants at the University hospital. In my few days here, I have been able to visit the excellent community health programme which has many different activities but is based on the concept of an integrated approach to health and development. An example of this is the groups of poor village girls employed in engineering work, in tailoring and embroidery and in the making of other handicrafts, all with the objective of gaining some income and being able to address the health needs of their families. Like St John's College, all the work is with women, and again they seem to have avoided many of the problems that we have had in working with young men. The community health work is comprehensive and of a very high standard. Of course, the University consists of much more than the community health department. There are nearly 70 departments of which about half are involved in teaching.*

*CMS has several mission partners here, and it was good to meet with them over a meal arranged by my hosts (Sara and Suranjan). Most of the CMS staff work in the Rehabilitation Department, which is headed by Suranjan. The rehabilitation work is really inspiring, and I thought of those with spinal injuries in Congo where there is very little help available. It made me more determined to support Sabuni in getting our degree in Community-Based Rehabilitation off the ground.*

*Apart from all I learned in Vellore, I appreciated the short break and*

*Sara and Suranjan's witness through their deep faith lived out in their simple lifestyle and their concern for the less privileged.*

*From India I returned to West Africa for several weeks, working in Bénin, and then finishing off the course at our new school in Côte d'Ivoire. From there I cross to East Africa with the hope of being in Nyankunde (Congo) with my colleagues for Christmas and the New Year.*

*News from Congo suggests that little has changed. The peace treaty signed a few months ago has not led to the withdrawal of rebels or foreign troops, and the tribal clashes to the north of Bunia have been very serious. However, it seems as though our colleagues have as much courage as before and are pushing on with the programme. The very urgent need is for buildings, but so far we have not been able to secure money for this. Please pray that a donor partner will understand and respond to this need.*

*During September, Sabuni, acting Director of IPASC, was with me in Liverpool. He had a reading month before beginning his PhD at Makerere University, Kampala. Nyangoma Kabarole, from Boga, was also in England having medical checks. We had a visit from Edouard Yao, my colleague in Côte d'Ivoire at the same time. With IPASC team members from Congo and Côte d'Ivoire present, we were able to have a useful 'Think-Tank' bringing together our advisers from Germany, our funding partners from Holland, a representative from the World Council of Churches, CMS and other friends of IPASC. This was a very helpful meeting as we looked at the structure needed to support both institutes and to co-ordinate their activities.*

*Nyangoma returned to Africa at the end of October and was admitted to Nairobi Hospital for peritoneal dialysis. Her sister, Elise,[24] stayed with her.*

### LL88: 20 April 2000

*Since my last letter, I have had seven weeks in England, much of which time was spent teaching at the Liverpool School of Tropical Medicine. I was happy to be able to visit in Colne and Silloth, and to catch up with friends in those parishes. There was also time to concentrate on strengthening the foundations of the* Institut Panafricain de Santé Communautaire (IPASC). *This is increasingly important as IPASC grows and increases its range of influence. Sustainability of the pro-*

gramme is a priority, and we need to be sure that we have made actual and contingency plans for the future. There are several ways in which this has been done:

## IPASC Advisory Group

In my last letter I mentioned the group of friends from St Mary's, Upton, Wirral (my parish church), who would be helping me to work through some of the management issues posed by the complexities of IPASC. This small group has been most helpful in getting me to be more focused, especially in areas that I find the most difficult to address. I was amazed how having a group to which I could refer made me more positive in tackling some of the problems, such as finance, that often gave me sleepless nights.

## An Administrative Assistant

One of the outcomes of the advisory group discussions was the appointment of an administrative assistant, based in the Wirral area (and a member of St Mary's). For the past four years I have carried my office around the world with me. My luggage has increasingly bulged with accounts and unanswered letters and reports, while my efficiency has deteriorated. Frequently urgent messages have circled round the globe looking for me, or sat at home patiently (or otherwise) waiting for a response! I arrive home to find hundreds (often over 500!) e-mails to answer, and you can imagine what impact that had on my enthusiasm to tackle administration as well as coping with a heavy lecture timetable at Liverpool and deputation at weekends. Now we have Mrs Jessie Hume, who has just retired from an important administrative job and still has plenty of energy, enthusiasm and initiative to put the IPASC 'mobile office' in order. Jessie joined the team (working part-time) at the beginning of April, and already I am feeling the enormous benefits. She knows where I am at any given time, and gets messages through to me immediately, but also copes with urgent problems. It is wonderful . . . and my luggage has lightened! In May I will be attending the World Health Assembly in Geneva and Jessie will meet me there and bring the 'office' with her, so we can discuss important issues. She will also have time to meet colleagues at WCC and WHO. The remaining baggage which circles the earth with me is the accounts – any offers or suggestions?!

*Friends of IPASC*
*Concurrent with the above developments, one of the Counsellors of the Liverpool School of Tropical Medicine, Mrs Rosemary Hawley, has promoted IPASC, and has been the force behind arrangements for presentations and lectures at the Liverpool School and has brought together interested people from the Diocese of Liverpool, the School of Tropical Medicine, the Merseyside Churches and local CMS members. A committee has been formed and activities (six-monthly) arranged. If you live in the Merseyside area and would like to know more about the Friends of IPASC you should contact Mrs Rosemary Hawley, The Rectory, Old Hall Lane, Kirkby, L32 5TH.*

*The Nyankunde Room*
*During my September lecturing period in Liverpool, I gave a lunch-time lecture to staff and students on developments at IPASC. Many had never known that IPASC existed, let alone that it had a close relationship with the School of Tropical Medicine. They were very interested. Later, while I was in Congo, the staff discussed the re-naming of the School's 'Old Museum' which has become a general purpose/social/exhibition room. It is large and spacious and is used daily. When it was suggested that it should be named the 'Ronald Ross Room' (after the scientist from the School of Tropical Medicine who discovered that certain mosquitoes were the vectors of malaria), a young, enthusiastic sociologist asked why such rooms were always dedicated to white, dead, male persons, and not to living persons/situations – such as Nyankunde! – and so it is that the Old Museum is now the 'Nyankunde Room' in recognition of the work of IPASC in the DR Congo! I was stunned and overwhelmed by this and by the plaque being prepared. It is an unmerited honour, yet at the same time I am so thrilled for my colleagues in DR Congo that all their hard work has been recognised. Our local artist in Nyankunde is now preparing three or four paintings of Nyankunde and IPASC to present to the School of Tropical Medicine, to hang in the Nyankunde Room.*

## LSTM

*The LSTM academic support for the work of IPASC was encouraging, and we were particularly grateful for a French-speaking colleague from Liverpool who ran several courses on epidemiology for District Medical*

*Officers. The Director visited us in Côte D'Ivoire, and other members of staff kept in touch. However, there was not the tangible link that I had hoped for, and so contact depended on personal relationships, which waned as those who had shared the original dream of IPASC began to move on. The naming of the common room at Liverpool, the 'Nyankunde Room', was a special gesture that I deeply appreciated, and there are several paintings of Nyankunde which were presented to Liverpool by IPASC.*

### LL89: 29 July 2000 – Moldova

*In my last letter I mentioned that I was planning to go to Moldova in May. The visit went ahead and was an eye-opener to the utter poverty in some of the newly independent states of eastern and central Europe. Health care is simply not accessible to most people, and now churches, Orthodox and Protestant, are recognising their need to develop a healing ministry within their communities.*

*IPASC has been asked to help with curriculum development for the Baptist Bible Institute in Kisinau, the capital, while there are many other potential openings for CMS.*

*Pat at her home in Nyankunde with baby Sammy Toko on her back, 1990s*

*Group of IPASC students studying herbal medicines, Nyankunde 1990s*

*IPASC staff and families, 2005*

*The green truck again, 2007*

*Chester-Aru-Boga Link visit, 2006*

*With Unega, 2007*

*With Esther Assia, 2007*

*Clergy colleagues at Upton St Mary's. Martin Daly, Pat, Graeme Skinner, 2007*

*Laura Arnold chatting to Pat,*
*Upton St Mary's Centre, 2007*

*Bishop Geoff Turner commissioning*
*Pat, Upton St Mary's Centre, 2007*

*Pat and Philippa Skinner,*
*last visit to Aru, 2008*

*With Alain Kaswera, last visit to Aru,*
*2008*

*With children, as usual, Aru, 2008*

*With MAF Pilot, 2008*

# CHAPTER 5

# Stories to Tell

As CMS moved into its bicentenary year (1999), I was attending a Conference for Universities in the poorest areas of the world, as a native Indian called upon the 'Grand Father' to *'give us strength: not that we be stronger than others, but rather that we share our strength with others'*. He reminded us that success was not about achieving, if achieving meant crossing the line first. Rather, we should not forget those we have left behind. In my life as a mission partner, who have I left behind? Where are the marginalised?

## Bunia Airport

In 2004, Bunia Airport was still a small, albeit international, airport. It was a place we knew well, having used it for our arrivals and departures from the country over the years. Most of the memories of it are mixed. It was the first experience of what corruption is like for visitors. Yet it was also the first experience of seeing how we, familiar with the staff there, became familiar with the strains on them, and the parameters within which they had to work to keep up some level of security and safety.

It was where the 'health officer', a nurse, would make his way to an incoming plane of five passengers, demanding, before passengers had time to collect their things together, their international health certificates. Off he would take them to his 'office' (a square foot of 'space' on the stone slab which made a 'bar' where refreshments were sold – if there were any). His task was not very lucrative (which meant that his salary was very limited) because most foreigners knew that smallpox was eradicated in 1979, were worried enough about yellow fever to have ensured they had had the immunisations, and had an international stamp. The one uncertainty for many naïve and intimidated travellers, cholera, was still a threat. Unfortunately, they had not realised that the immunisation against cholera had long been taken off the list of international requirements, so depending how vulnerable the passenger looked, a 'fine' was charged for breaking international health laws. Of course it was a negotiable fine, so may have started at $20 but could have been reduced considerably if the passenger was more experienced in haggling than coping with international health laws, and had the time to haggle. One thing that did not enter the negotiations was the offer of an immunisation, because there were seldom any available (and the nurse recognised that most foreigners had been warned against 'dirty needles' at other airports).

Waiting for a plane at Bunia Airport could mean a long wait, and there was very little to do, unless one had a book to read. Some of us wandered across to the Anglican Theological College (ISThA) just ten minutes away, to wait in comfort (but at risk of the plane landing without one's knowledge). On more than one occasion, I waited outside, at the back of the airport, where it was quieter and cooler.

## Dhenzama

Dhenzama came from a poor home and had not been able to complete the education that her widowed mother was struggling to provide for her. She left school to help care for the home, though years later had some basic nursing training. However, in the 1990s, the Government remodelled the nursing training, eliminating the basic nursing certificate and the qualification that it carried. Those holding the certificate could no longer be employed, leaving excellent grass-roots workers such as Dhenzama without usable qualifications, and thus without work. It also left the communities without some of their most precious and committed workers.

Recognising the waste to poorer families as well as to the community, IPASC gave priority admission to people like Dhenzama, though was aware that it would be a struggle for them to cope with the higher academic level of the diploma course. In collaboration with the Ministry of Health's training department, modifications were made to emphasise their practical skills of training. Dhenzama struggled with French and with complicated subjects such as pharmacology, and there was constant discouragement when exams had to be repeated, and, following State regulations for all examinations, with a perpetual threat of failure after two attempts at each exam. The additional burden of finding fees, and, as a single parent, being concerned for her child being cared for by Granny hundreds of miles away, just poured on the pressure for Dhenzama. Plump, considerably older than other students, from a poor village background where social skills were very different from those of the younger generation, Dhenzama was fighting many battles. However, she had a strong faith and, when it came to practical work, she was a different person, helped considerably by her previous experience as a community nurse-midwife. Her relationship with those who suffered discrimination for various reasons was outstanding.

During a tribal war in her own village of Blukwa, Dhenzama alone kept the health centre open when others fled for safety. A night-time attack on the village by an unknown group of militia brought total chaos and confusion. Many of the villagers were severely injured by the marauding militia, who were raping as they pilfered the mud huts, and carried off the wares of village traders. Amongst it all, women in labour and others admitted with malaria and other diseases needed attention, though Dhenzama was alone. She tried to reduce further hardship by taking those from a particularly vulnerable tribe into her own home, although her own family was mourning the loss of several of its members in a previous attack on the village. Her return to Nyankunde to continue with her studies was no less dramatic.

For the fourth year of her training (a practical year) Dhenzama was sent to another conflict 'hot spot' at Iga Barrier, a traditional gold-mining area. It was considered that she was the only person who could handle Iga Barrier which was situated at an important crossroads where commercial, mining, tribal and power interests cascaded into a kaleidoscope of tension and fighting. Not long after her arrival there, the health centre became home to a mass of displaced people looking for safety from the marauding rebels. With the intention of giving Dhenzama a break from such a tense and dangerous situation, it was suggested that she spend the last few months of her training in a quieter village. However, the villagers appealed that she be left at Iga Barrier, claiming that no one else was capable of doing her job. The church which was responsible for the health centre immediately appointed her as Nurse-in-Charge of the health centre, although she was still a student (albeit at the end of her training), because they were determined that Dhenzama remain with them. Dhenzama passed her four-year State Diploma as a community midwife with distinction – not because of any academic achievements, but because of her total commitment to and ability with the community where she had saved many lives. Two years later, the health centre was upgraded by the District Medical Officer to be a reference centre (offering a full range of health care and community health services). It was thanks to Dhenzama's leadership that, a little later, IPASC was able to recommend Iga Barrier Health Centre to Tearfund for a grant to rebuild some of the war damage and the loss of equipment. Thanks to Dhenzama's work, the health district of Iga Barrier Health Centre was one of nine districts selected to be partnered by IPASC in community health activities. Dhenzama visits IPASC in Aru frequently, dipping into and borrowing resources, sharing her experiences with staff and students, and just being part of the IPASC family. She is an example of the treasure that could so easily have been discarded by the upgrading of Government training and practice.

### Unega (Unega Djamiem: book-keeper)

Before becoming a member of staff at IPASC, Unega worked in the staff shop at the Christian Medical Centre (CME) at Nyankunde. Unega was a real gentleman – he benefited from a good general education at a Christian School, where he showed a love for listening to classical music from the missionaries. As he gained experience as a family man, so he developed a vision for the potential within village communities.

By 1994, IPASC was growing, and the tasks (big and small) for which I was responsible were far too many. For example, I did not take sufficient time or care with the cash I was holding and I often forgot to write down how I was using the money. Life was moving too fast for me, and I never got it right. As always, I shared my problem with Mama Sheri over the lunch table. As always, she had just the right answer. 'Papa Unega is the person you need.' At the time, Unega was filling in for someone on holiday at the staff shop. It was hard to be patient, but I had to agree that if Unega was right for us, we would wait for him. I could try to do better for three weeks, so long as we had the right person. Good book-keeping was going to be essential to IPASC, though little did we know how large the programme was to grow and how essential the role of 'book-keeper' was to become.

Unega had a growing family, and was already one of the older members of staff. He was well known in the church community and was someone whom the local community depended on for development ideas. For example, he was key, in his village, to the establishment and maintenance of a funeral club – a group of families who shared the burden of funeral costs as a co-operative, and used the club for other development such as health education for member families. It was that sort of outside experience that made Unega so special as IPASC developed its own vision for work in communities. While nothing to do with book-keeping, it was often Unega who gently but firmly put forward workable and innovative ideas. He was one of the first to really understand the concept of 'obusinge' and he used it so much in his own work, in his home and among the staff, that he was a real inspiration to others.

Despite having no professional training, Unega was able to take a valuable part in discussing some of the academic aspects of IPASC's development, while also bringing out his community experience. He married the two together, which was more difficult for those with higher education who often forgot or ignored the community context of IPASC's work.

As a senior staff member, but still the book-keeper and the one sensitive to the needs of the community, with tremendous support, and maybe some whispered advice from his wife, Unega could be found at all hours of the day or night, at his book-keeping. But just as often he would gently come and stand by my side, 'I've been thinking . . . ' he would begin. 'Let's go and sit down', would be my reply as I expected another wise idea. In the idea that was about to be launched, I knew that Unega would have been listening to the community again, perhaps with a new idea about a water source or hygiene problem, or other development in the community. What a privilege to have such rough diamonds, who shine in the community, on the staff and in the cash office, and who are special brothers and sisters in Christ.

## Rehema

Rehema, aged 23, delivered her fourth child normally in a rural health centre on 8 April. One previous child died at birth; the eldest is 28 months old and with severe malnutrition, and the toddler of eleven months is pathetically small. Two days after the delivery the nurses decided (too late) that Rehema was very anaemic. They asked the relatives to carry her to Nyankunde Hospital. When the family went to pay the bill, the staff at the health centre refused the £8 and two goats saying that the family should keep these for the bill they would have to pay at Nyankunde. Having left the health centre, the family first returned home. They looked for young men to carry Rehema the fifteen miles to Nyankunde, but no one was available. Rehema waited a week, losing strength each day. Eventually, as her breathing became more difficult, a team of men was formed and carried her through the night on an improvised stretcher. She died a few hours later! We need to help nurses to make earlier diagnosis, and families to understand that an emergency needs a rapid response. Both of these issues means improved communications, and this is one of our objectives.

## IPASC green Toyota pickup

IPASC was blessed to have the Toyota pickup from the Chichester Diocese in the United Kingdom. The vehicle itself has a story to tell. As the only vehicle that IPASC had at that period, it was of great help in IPASC's activities. The vehicle started its real story in 1996 when the first war started, the one opposing late President Mobutu's regime. As soldiers were hunting vehicles, the green pickup was to be taken to its first refuge place. It was hidden far in the forest, where they had to dig the hole and cover it with banana leaves. When the war was over, the car was taken out in 1997, and taken back to its refuge place again in 1998, when the RCD movement (Congolese Rally for Democracy) started its war against the Kabila regime. In 1999, the car was brought to Bunia where IPASC started its college university in November 1998.

From 1999 to 2003 the green pickup went through a number of traumatic experiences in Bunia, as it was a period characterised by ethnic fightings. The situation was getting worse as the militias were after every car they could find. We decided with the IPASC management team in Bunia to hide the car at one of the staff member's homes, where they could not easily tell if there was a car around. In 2003, especially between February and May, when the situation really got worse, we decided to take out different major parts of the car, including tyres. The green pickup was just put on stones, meaning to other people that the car was completely broken down. In May 2003, we had to leave Bunia, because there was no way of enduring any more. We left the car on stones where it was kept. As the situation was cooling down, the management committee of IPASC decided to take the car to Aru so that it could be used to help in some field activities. The main question was how, because militias were still active in Bunia and they were still looting people's vehicles.

Amuda Baba tells the story. 'In September 2003, I was sent to Bunia to explore the possibility of taking that car out of the town. As we arrived, we made contact with the mechanics who undid the green pickup so that they could fix it again, where it was taking its refuge. They had to make it quietly, not even starting it, because militias were moving around. We brought six mechanics and they worked for a full day, from 6am to 5pm. Meanwhile, we collected some books that had been brought by the watchmen, in sacks on bicycles, from IPASC University College (where they had been thrown out by militias who forced all of the building doors) to where the vehicle was kept along with the IPASC photocopying machine. We put them at the back of the green vehicle. At 5pm, Pate, a friend of mine, started the car and drove it at high speed and hid it in a container at his boss's compound in Bunia town. While the car was in the container, we were making arrangements with some aviation companies to help us take the car to Entebbe in Uganda. An aviation company accepted to take the car. But how were we going to take the car to the airport? The aviation company told us to get ready and they were going to tell us when to take the car to the airport. At 4.30pm, they called us. Before leaving, we just prayed that God would help us through, as the road heading to the airport was one of the most dangerous. Pate started the car, and we went at high speed to the airport. When we were passing, we could see that people were very astonished, asking themselves how did they really manage to hide that car and where did they hide it? Unfortunately, it was too late for them. The car was taken into an Antonov aeroplane. At around 5.15pm, the plane took off, and I just said 'Thank you Lord.'

Arriving at Entebbe International Airport in Uganda an hour later (7.15pm Ugandan local time), we left everything in the plane and had to leave for Kampala. The following day, we went back to Entebbe with a Ugandan driver so that they could provide some essential documents to allow the car to be driven in Uganda. That day, we left Entebbe at 5.30pm and drove to Kampala, where the vehicle was to be fixed, because what was done in Bunia was just for emergency use. After three days in Kampala, we left and were heading now to Aru, via Vurra. We were in touch with Elias, who mobilised himself to wait for us in Vurra, on the Ugandan border with DR Congo. We managed to reach Vurra at 3.30pm where we found Elias waiting for us. Then Elias drove the car from Vurra to Aru. When we arrived in Aru, we found a number of IPASC staff members who were eagerly waiting to see their green pickup. We could see how people were happy, smiling and everyone surrounding the car, touching it, trying to talk to it. Then a thanksgiving prayer was said, when everyone stood around that car.

Since then, the car is doing a great job to support operational programmes in Aru.'

## *LL71: May–June 1995*

*Our buildings are growing, and our present course is going well with 30 students. The planning for our first English course in Uganda (September) is well under way, and is already fully booked. Departmentalisation has enabled me to share my responsibilities between four departments, and this has been a tremendous help, and has reminded me how privileged I am to be part of a very competent team.*

*There's a sense of progress when one is able to respond to real needs, rather than just teaching. 'Operation IPASC' has seen the mobilisation of IPASC students in a massive effort to curtail the cholera epidemic which has recently hit the Nyankunde health district. Students and staff mixed the need for experience in epidemiology with their expertise in communicating health messages, to cover the whole District. Faida (our 'reporter', and also a lecturer), covered the operation on video, getting into situations where a foreign reporter would never be allowed. We are delighted that the number of new cases of cholera has reduced dramatically this week. Another important 'campaign' is the reduction of deaths of women during pregnancy and childbirth. At present the number of women dying is alarming, and most of these deaths are preventable.*

## *LL73: November 1995*

*Many of you prayed with us as Dr François Mwema and his family prepared to leave Liverpool to join us at IPASC. They have now been with us for six weeks, and are beginning to adapt to the situation. Although they are originally from Zaïre, there is a lot to re-learn. The older children still speak better English than anything else (complete with a Liverpool accent!), but are attending a French school (and English Sunday School). Like new mission partners, they are falling prey to local illnesses. We are delighted to have the Mwemas with us, but continue to pray for them during this difficult time of re-adjusting to life in Zaïre.*

## LL74: May–July 1996

### Madagascar

I attended the opening of the Africa Evangelical Fellowship's new hospital at Mandritsara, in the north of the country. We have been associated with the programme through Dr Adrien Ralaimiarison, one of IPASC's Board members – a Malagasy surgeon who spent some time with his family at Nyankunde. There is a real hope here that they will soon be able to get a community health programme started. However, there is a shortage of trained personnel or even potential candidates for training. This beautiful large Indian Ocean island is neither African nor Asian (or is both) but has its own unique characteristics and needs. There are many Christian denominations in the country. Even in the little town of Mandritsara I found a tin shack called the 'Anglican Church' apparently playing that role on Sundays because it doubled as a radio repair shop during the week. CMS has had mission partners working with the Anglican Church in Madagascar.

### Boga

From Madagascar I went straight to Boga for the centenary of the Anglican Church in Zaïre. What a wonderful occasion that was! There were friends from many countries joining to celebrate the arrival in Boga of Canon Apolo Kivebulaya (the 'African Saint'), who had come from Uganda. He was the first missionary of the Anglican Church in the old Belgian Congo (now Zaïre – and then DR Congo). The highlight for me was the student nurses' enactment of the life of Apolo – which enabled us to travel, suffer and rejoice as his pioneer missionary steps were retraced. It was certainly a challenge to us modern mission partners, with e-mail and computers and an apparent lack of time to spend with people, just sharing the love of Jesus. On the Sunday, we split up into a number of groups and took different paths that Apolo would have walked to visit the parishes that he established. At each cluster of homes we stopped, shared and received the Gospel and prayed with those who had gathered. Many came forward to commit or recommit their lives to Christ, or to ask for prayer for peace or healing. During the walk I met many old friends, and it was a wonderful reminder of the years I had spent in that very special community. I spent four days at home at Nyankunde, where we hosted a seminar for Tearfund partners in Zaïre.

## Western Ethiopia

*During a three-week visit to Western Ethiopia I have been evaluating the Mekene Yesus Church's Health Programmes and focusing on the work of the community health workers (who have a strong sense of social service or religious motivation). For example: in the Bodji area of Ethiopia over 100 church deacons serve as unpaid community health volunteers.*[26]

*I always feel ambivalent about long periods of travel. It creates enormous administrative problems and a lack of continuity in our IPASC teaching programme. It's exhausting and I know that I will be even more tired when I get back to Nyankunde because there will be so much to catch up on. My dog sums up my feelings by his reaction to seeing my suitcase being packed. He sits on top of it looking very forlorn – though all is forgiven when I return home!*

## LL81: 14 September 1998

*The severe cholera epidemic that began in April 1998 dragged on. During the worst of the epidemic, IPASC played a co-ordination role. Thanks to help from several organisations and friends, and the partnership of the pilots working with the Mission Aviation Fellowship (and based at Nyankunde), we were able to keep up a constant supply of intravenous fluids, respond immediately to calls from medical personnel and keep the death rates low. This meant sending up to three small planes a day, full of IV fluids, to the worst of the areas, or getting our students out to isolated villages to set up cholera camps. I travelled a great deal during that time, trying to encourage weary staff, check on the management of large cholera camps and assess the progress of the epidemic. Our students became cholera experts.*

*As a result of our experience, we hope to establish a rapid response team, able to respond to any crisis, rather than just cholera. One impact of our work was the breaking down of barriers between Catholics and Protestants. Cholera certainly does not make a difference between ethnic or religious groups. Working with all the teams was a joy to us and a support and sense of fellowship to the various missions with whom we worked, and continue to be associated. Our links with the Government, which were already good, were also strengthened.*

*Into my kaleidoscope come some grey scenes. Usually very fit, the last few months have taken me through the 'valleys' of malaria and typhus.*

*Unfortunately, both occurred at difficult and busy times. I tried to cope, but found myself thinking that a hospital bed might be more comfortable than trying to soldier on! Times like this can be very lonely, so I am thankful that they do not happen too often.*

*They discovered the epicentre of the epidemic (as well as discovering many other major health problems). Now we have to do something about it, hopefully with some expert help from our colleagues at the Liverpool School of Tropical Medicine.*

## LL84: 24 June 1999

*Elias' graduation*

*One occasion I missed was the national celebration on Clapham Common. On Saturday 29 May, I woke up to the thought that CMS friends from all over England would soon be making their way to Clapham for the splendid anniversary celebrations – a day which promised to be full and exciting finishing with Haydn's 'Creation'. I was so sorry not to be there – but, at the same time, glad to be in Nairobi and able to attend Elias' graduation (BA in Business Management). Elias is a staff member[25] from IPASC, Congo, who has been studying in Nairobi. It was a wonderful day! We brought roses for Elias (an African custom) and as he graduated we (friends and colleagues from DR Congo including Sabuni), surged towards him with an abundance of congratulations . . . and then Elias' name was called again – he was awarded a special prize for his 'leadership and community involvement'. I felt as proud as a mother! After the ceremony the 'IPASC family' went out for a meal to celebrate. It was almost like being back in Nyankunde, as we shared together all that had been happening. There was lots of good news – 85 students in the first year of the new university course, all staff continuing enthusiastically, despite the difficulties . . . but bad news too – Gertrude died from drinking potent home-made alcohol – leaving three orphaned sons; a student died while working in a rebel area where he could not reach medical help when he became sick. Also, tragically, one of our Board members – Father Oscar (an Argentinean doctor/priest/missionary) died suddenly in Congo, a couple of weeks ago, probably of malaria. This was a blow. Fr Oscar had such a meaningful ministry, and was a good friend and colleague.*

*Sabuni*

There was a very touching story from Congo. Sabuni, acting in my place as Director, had been frustrated because we had not been able to get funding to construct the new university buildings. Until now the Bible School in Bunia has lent IPASC some of their buildings, but Sabuni and colleagues were worried that there was not enough room to accommodate all the students, and he did not like them having to wander through the rebel-held town after classes. So he told the rest of the staff that he would buy some tin roofing with his own money, and that they would all work towards putting up a mud dormitory. The other staff members followed his example, each paying for one or two pieces of iron sheeting each month (£5 apiece – and 80 pieces were needed). The average staff salary is £60 a month! The mud dormitory is now nearing completion, and the students will have at least a temporary place to stay in – thanks to the generosity of the staff.

Would the staff of an institute in England sacrifice 10–15% of their salary for a few months so that their students had safe accommodation? I am sure this would not have happened had I been there, and I praise God for Sabuni's initiative. Please pray that funding for the buildings will be forthcoming. Following the graduation, Sabuni came back to Abidjan to help me with some management problems. He was excellent, and coped with issues that I was finding particularly difficult. I was so grateful for his help.

Since my leaving Congo at the beginning of the present war (August 1998), Sabuni has developed leadership skills and much wisdom (some good things come out of long separations!). Professor Molyneux, Director of the Liverpool School of Tropical Medicine, visited our work in Abidjan while Sabuni was still with us. He was very pleased to meet Sabuni (who had done a Master's degree at Liverpool) again, and was delighted with the IPASC site at Mafiblé, just to the east of Abidjan, nestling among the coconuts, by a large lagoon. We discussed the potential of the two IPASCs (Congo and Côte d'Ivoire) and their role in working with churches, governments and international organisations. The question is whether or not we have the staff and the resources to be able to cope with all the opportunities opening up to us.

It is this ever-increasing potential of IPASC that has led Sabuni and me to look carefully at our support structure. We need to be sure that we have the resources, not only financial, but more particularly *professional and managerial, to be able to cope. My main concern is that we need more points of reference – more advisers to challenge, stimulate and guide us. Maybe we need to form a Trust or seek recognition as a charity in England, so that we can ensure our sustainability as an ecumenical team, addressing some of the major issues of quality of care in church-related health programmes. But I do not know to whom I should turn.*

*Who could provide the managerial, legal and professional advice that we need? If you know of anyone (including yourselves!) experienced in the legal and/or managerial aspects of charitable organisations or trusts, please let us know. Please make this a point of prayer.*

*Revisiting Nyankunde, 2008*

*With Faida, 2008*

*Philippa and Pat with Bishop Isingoma, 2008*

*Pat's retirement from St Mary's Upton staff team, 2009*

*Remy and Annette Toko at LSTM for dedication of
Nickson Room, 30 January 2010*

*Professor Janet Hemingway unveiling memorial at
LSTM, 30 January 2010*

*2009 – still talking about IPASC*

# CHAPTER 6

# Conflict and War Punctuate Health Development (1993–2003)

*LL64: 13 February 1993*

*Bénin, Mali, Cameroun and Tchad. It went very well indeed. The situation in DRC is chaotic and insecure with fighting in Kinshasa (because salaries were not paid), during which the French Ambassador was killed. Many people fled the country, including Europeans who were evacuated from Kinshasa. Constant messages were transmitted by the BBC from the Foreign Office warning expatriates to leave Kinshasa (I had my own warning by fax!). Since then the President has sacked the Prime Minister, we have no government or parliament at the moment. The Kinshasa problems have not affected us directly, but indirectly have contributed to the increasing instability in the country, and the anarchical tendency. In the east of the country the main problem has been looting by troops of villages and towns. Several missionary families, colleagues of ours, lost everything, but continued with their work. Rebel attacks have continued, though have moved away from the Boga area to towns on the Ugandan border, about 100 miles further south.*

*At the beginning of February a new crisis arose, on top of everything else. Tribal fighting erupted with a vengeance, all around us. At first it was confined to a specific area, about twelve miles from Nyankunde. Many men, women and children were killed, and we saw the results of brutal butchery at the hospital. Because the trouble seemed to be so localised, I flew to Boga last weekend (5–8 February) . . .*

*Despite all the drama of the second course, it got off to a good start on 1 February 1993.*

*Unfortunately, the first course was peppered with periods of insecurity in the Ituri Region, but this did not alarm the students, most of whom had had similar experiences in their own countries. Nevertheless, as the numbers of dead and injured rose in the community, many villagers ran into the bush while others stayed to protect fields and homes, making the logistics of village work, especially in the Boga area, very difficult. Nyakato Kabarole was amazing in her capacity as Development Officer of the Diocese of Boga, and managed to control the effects of rebel insurgencies sufficiently to prevent the normal complications of rape and corruption. I went to Boga several times during this difficult period, both as a friend and as an ongoing staff member of the Diocesan health board. One evening, after supper, about 50 Ngety[27] from nearby villages came to the house for safety, carrying the few belongings they had grabbed as they ran from their burning homes. Some had already lost family members, especially children, when burning grass roofs fell on them. Others had not lost their homes, but had run in terror at the approaching militia attacks. Somehow, in the two hours that followed, all 50 were fed, bathed and found some floor space for a bed at Nyakabale.*

*I was challenged by the courage and faith of friends like Nyangoma. They worked tirelessly, disregarding tribal differences, and showing nothing but love. What did I do? I am ashamed to say that I lay on my comfortable bed feeling very frightened! I could hear the men of the village who were on guard out on the surrounding hills, calling to one another, and giving what information they could glean from those nearer the villages in trouble. Even some of the women were there, keeping watch. Around midnight came word that the fighting would not reach Boga. The Chief of Boga came round to tell us to go to bed as he had scouts out everywhere. The next day, Sunday, seemed calm in the morning. The cathedral was packed for the morning service, at which the Archbishop preached on love and peace, pleading to the Christian community not to let the problems infect their relationships. The peace between Christians of different tribes was moving as they shared their one-ness while their brothers were killing one another. I had been invited out to lunch with one of the pastors, but the excellent meal was interrupted by the Chief's drum. Through all my years in Boga I have known about the special drum, and how it is used only in times of real danger. Now it was being used to call all able-bodied men into action to defend their villages, and women to guard their families. The atmosphere was electric; the reaction was immediate. Without a word, the men reached for their spears (many would hardly ever have used them before) and ran. Everyone knew exactly what to do, as though they had been drilled over the years. I made for the Archbishop's house with the children, as men rushed past saying to me, 'It's bad Mama, it's very bad.' I prayed silently for them, as I tried to hurry the children, who thought this was great fun! Before we got to the Archbishop's house we were met by Nyangoma in the hospital Land Rover. She had thrown some things together – we could not go home – and was driving as quickly as possible to Tchabi, twelve miles (45 minutes) away to leave us there and alert the military commander that urgent help was needed.*

*That night at Tchabi there must have been nearly a hundred of us, each person concerned for family and friends left behind, and for their homes. The next day, crowds more people arrived from Boga. I was picked up by an MAF plane to return to Nyankunde, where I needed to get on with work at IPASC, but it was tough leaving the family and friends at Boga. As we flew over Boga, the devastation below was grotesque. There were fires all around, but at Mitego (five miles from Boga) it looked as though the village had been wiped out a few days before, with only the charred remains of the huts left. Later we heard that there were about 6,000 displaced people at Boga, more at Tchabi, and others hiding in the bush. Thirty miles away there were other large pockets of refugees and at Nyankunde there were many, many more – though a large number of people had evacuated to Bunia, which was full of displaced people, and was also coping with different groups of disgruntled soldiers. Prices had rocketed because there was so little food about (nobody was harvesting the fields, and people were frightened to travel to sell their food at markets).*

### *LL65: 1993*

*The general political and economic situation of the country remains unchanged – except that, at present, we have two prime ministers, and no one is sure who, if anyone, is in control! Meanwhile, anarchy reigns supreme, particularly among the military personnel, and at the cost of villagers. Our immediate problem was a spin-off from the general state of the country. With little infrastructure, local problems can, and did, get out of control.*

*The tribal war between the Wahema and Wangiti tribes had its roots in a long-standing dispute about land-ownership, colour being added* to the original conflict by church differences. The area involved included Nyankunde, but almost excluded Boga (except a few nasty incidents), though Boga has borne the brunt of the problem of thousands of displaced persons who have sought sanctuary there.

The light of the church shone, and still shines from Boga – thanks to Archbishop Njojo, Nyangoma and Nyakato Kabarole, Rev Katabuka and other remarkable people in the diocesan team. For a month they have been feeding over 4,000 people, many of whom have lost their homes, their belongings and, in some cases, their loved ones. Here at Nyankunde the problem was different. The referral hospital here received a number of very seriously injured patients from the fighting – some gun-shot wounds, but mostly, mutilation from sheer butchery. Very quickly the meagre 'poor fund' was emptied, and yet we had patients everywhere, and their whole families with them (since most had lost their homes). A hospital like this is not equipped to look after refugees. However, the medical and general staff did their utmost for these severely traumatised folk.

Today, a team of our IPASC students has gone out to evaluate the damage to all the health centres in the area. Nyankunde and Boga have collaborated closely in the relief efforts, and Nyangoma is with me at present. She has been buying cloth, hoes (so people can prepare fields before the rains come in a week or two), and food. Wherever possible our strategies have been towards rapid rehabilitation – not easy with people who have suffered so, and seek only sanctuary!

The present situation is one of uneasy calm. There is little trust around, particularly here at Nyankunde. There are repeated efforts at reconciliation, prayer meetings, and interventions from civic authorities (such as they are), but one side is not ready to trust the other. Despite all the trauma, there have been lighter moments for us. Only yesterday, Nyangoma and I went out with some students to a remote village where there are several thousand displaced people. To get to the village we had to cross a traditional forest bridge made of ropey twines, swung high across a fast-flowing river (as seen in 'Tarzan'!). We pretended to be brave, but the precarious swaying bridge, fast-flowing river a long way beneath, and little to catch hold of, almost defeated us. Later we re-named the bridge 'Pont de Nyangoma', since Nyangoma found it more of a challenge than living in Liverpool for two years!

The hospital has had its own dramas apart from the war. Some weeks ago a man was brought down from the Central African Republic by MAF. He had been mauled by a lion, and had very serious head and facial injuries. Dr Albert Ahuka is a superb surgeon and, thanks to his skill, and to God's grace, the patient is alive, and relatively well. However, he still needs much more surgery. He and his son came without anything, and over £500 has already been spent on the patient's hospital care! About the same time as the accident involving the lion (during which five other people were killed), an American lady was attacked by a crocodile, and needed an amputation of an arm. The outcome of the story of the lion is that the patient was kept at Nyankunde for a year while his very serious injuries were healing. He went home somewhat disfigured, but having been cared for by Christians, including some of IPASC's students from his area who could speak his language. They will remain in contact with the family back in Central African Republic.

I am very grateful for a particularly good group of students at IPASC. They have done well, and the staff have proved a tower of strength.

## LL66: 1993

African sunsets are special! Regardless of all the trials and tribulations of a day, the sounds, scents, colours of dusk speak of the beauty all around.

The situation in Zaïre continues to deteriorate, with several areas of severe tribal fighting, near anarchy among the military, and absolute poverty in most communities. Devaluation continues at about 7% a day and most of us have stopped trying to count in the local currency. No shops or market are open. Trading soap for sweet potatoes or whatever is in the field sometimes helps. We have all been hungry and we have not been able to pay salaries, but giving food where possible. Nyangoma sends me food from Boga. Airports are closed and insecurity increasing – just when District Medical Officers seminars have been given! Borders are closed. Complicating all the difficulties at the moment is an epidemic of meningitis, which is attacking both adults and children, with about half of the cases admitted to the hospital dying within a few days. Of those who recover, many will have cerebral damage, including permanent deafness. We are looking for ways of getting vaccine from Kenya, and immunising the most vulnerable. Despite all the problems there is tremendous courage among the people.

*We have so much to learn from them; from their faith; and from their happiness in the simplest things of life.*

## LL67: November–December 1993

*I wonder if you are preparing for Christmas? Have you ordered your turkey, bought Christmas crackers, or started to send cards? Despite our very different situation, I think we are going to experience some of the concerns and joys of the First Christmas. This short letter is in lieu of a card, and comes with warm greetings from Zaïre.*

*I suppose my mental preparations for Christmas began this week, when, suddenly, all missionaries had to report to their nearest civic authorities for a census of foreigners. We had very little notice, and overnight had to rearrange plans, mobilise all the vehicles and MAF aeroplanes, and get ourselves into Bunia (28 miles away, but a two-hour drive). At IPASC we have ten foreign students (from Togo, Cameroun, Rwanda and Central African Republic, so we all packed into one Land Rover). It was a hot day, and we were all tired, dusty and fed-up by the time we arrived in Bunia. Imagine what it would have been like to do the journey on a donkey, and towards the end of a pregnancy!*

*Sadly, here in Zaïre, nobody can prepare special food for Christmas. In fact, to prepare enough food for today is an enormous problem for us all. The situation is very difficult. In the past two weeks the economy has deteriorated even faster than before. The present exchange rate is anything between 30 million–60 million Zaïres/$1. The currency is being changed (1 new Zaïre = 3 million old Zaïres), but there is no money about. There are no shops or market stalls open, or village women selling! The only way we can buy vegetables is by trading salt or soap for beans or sweet potatoes. All of us have been hungry. Nyangoma keeps sending vegetables for me from Boga, and we are all sharing everything we have. We cannot pay salaries, but have been giving what food we have to our staff. How can I keep feeding my dog when so many people have nothing? Perhaps, in a different context, these were some of the concerns that Joseph and Mary had to contend with, as they anticipated the birth of their child.*

*Insecurity is a perpetual problem for us, as in so many African countries at this time. The airports in Zaïre are closed, and the only way of getting in or out of the country is by crossing the road border with*

*Uganda at Aru. Imagine! For us, this could not have come at a worse time. Beginning tomorrow, we have two important seminars for 25 district medical officers, each of which lasts one week. Immediately afterwards we have our annual Administrative Council, and a conference for those working in church-related health programmes from many African French-speaking countries. What do we do? The borders are closed, there is no money, and no food; but did Joseph and Mary lose courage or give up when so much was against them?*

*Perhaps this is the Christmas message of joy for us: nobody here is giving up. My colleagues have been tremendously courageous in taking each problem as it has come, and handing it back to God. Their courage has been rewarded with blessings, and we feel as though our cruse of oil is still supplying our needs. I have learned a great deal through this experience . . . I expect Joseph and Mary did too ('she bore all these things in her heart')! May you have joys and blessings this Christmas, and bear in your hearts all the encouragements which come through handing things back to God. Wishing you all joy and peace this Christmas.*

### LL68: 20 June 1994

*I am sure that many of you have been disturbed by the pictures you are seeing on television of the genocide in Rwanda. During the past month, this ghastly situation has changed my life and my priorities.*

*When the war broke out in Rwanda we became very concerned for Rwandan friends. I felt very helpless, and asked God to show me how we could be used in the situation. However, a day or two later, the senior pilot informed me that I would be receiving about twelve visitors the following day. 'I think they may be refugees from Rwanda' he added. The following day twelve Rwandans, including Bishop Samuel Habiamana, arrived in a small plane but he left immediately, saying, 'I'm going back for more.' The following day another planeload arrived. I now had 20 visitors in my little home – all of whom had been very severely traumatised. They were a mixture of Hutu and Tutsi, of adults and children, and all in need of love and understanding. They were also in need of food, clothes and beds! 'Why', I asked myself, 'did the Bishop bring them here and not to the refugee camp?' Twenty refugees invading my privacy, my home, my everything, was a bit too much! Then I heard their story – and dropped to my knees to ask for forgiveness for my selfish attitude.*

*I have never seen WCC move so fast, but within two days arrangements had been made to form a team for the Zairean camps from 'my family', together with my own staff from IPASC. A budget and terms of reference were drawn up for a three-week evaluation of their needs and our resources. I will return to Zaïre almost immediately (27 June), but I expect to be back in Geneva at the end of July for debriefing of this initial phase and to present a longer-term programme which we will have worked out in Zaïre. Our team is to be called the African Community Initiative Support Team, Zaïre (ACIST-Z). The main objective of ACIST is to enable communities in the camps in Goma, Butembo and Uvira to define their priorities in the rehabilitation process, and to facilitate their achieving their priorities by making resources available to them. You may see news of other ACIST teams for the other countries bordering Rwanda. Ours will be the first off the ground, so we will be carefully monitored so that others can learn from us. However, before we can help the thousands of refugees, we need to be sure that 'our family' members have had time, and the help they need, for their own recovery.*

## LL69: 28 July 1994

*The events of the past month have been indescribable. Politico-ethnic antagonism reached a climax in Rwanda following the deaths of the Rwandan and Burundian presidents in a plane crash in April, and resulted in the slaughter of hundreds of thousands of Rwandans. Most of those who survived fled to neighbouring countries. Of a population of 6.5 million in the tiny country of Rwanda, probably as many as 1 million were killed, and 4 million are refugees. Of the refugees, over 2 million are in Eastern Zaïre, mostly in and around the town of Goma.*

*In my last letter, I shared the World Council of Churches' plan to send teams into the refugee camps to provide community support – often an element which is lacking in the aid given to refugees. We were a team of four – Bishop Samuel Musabyiamana (Bishop of the Diocese of Shyogwe, Rwanda), Mme Esperence (a young widow from Kigali), Pasteur Kolongi from Bukavu, and myself, and our brief was to evaluate the needs of the camps south of Goma, and then to liaise with another team in Goma.*

*We arrived in Bukavu on 4 July, and began work straight away. This was not difficult as there were refugees everywhere. The Bishop's compound, where we stayed, was already overflowing with people. We visited camps, and worked among people sheltering in the town. On several occasions we visited Rwanda, always under French military protection, flying in helicopters and military transport planes. On one occasion we met with church leaders at the lakeside town of Kibuye (Rwanda) and established a relief project which Tearfund would have supported – but the church leaders who would have been responsible for the project fled a few days later. We met old friends and strangers, all desperate for a degree of hope.*

*Both in the camps in Zaïre, and in Rwanda, there were very many traumatised people. A number had hands or fingers missing, many had machete wounds, while others were totally dazed and unable to hold a conversation. There was very little food available in Rwanda, but the French were sharing their own rations with the people they were protecting. During one of our visits to Rwanda, a mother arrived exhausted at the French military camp. Her husband had been killed during the night, and she had escaped with her baby, leaving four other children alone in the house. I was given charge of the baby for a couple of hours, while the French took the mother in an armoured vehicle to look for the other children. There were sad times, and very frightening times, but I was glad that we were able to make those visits to Rwanda to remind people that the church cared.*

*We found that the needs of the people in the many camps we visited in Zaïre were similar: a more varied diet (only beans and maize are given – which is not a Rwandan diet); health care and especially primary health care (one woman sold her food allowance to be able to pay to have her baby in a health centre); recreational/occupational activities; toilet facilities and a building/tent for worship. We found very many traumatised refugees. I will never forget the haunting face of a lonely widow, with two small children. She looked old, but could only have been about thirty. She was exhausted and thin, and very frightened. She had watched her husband and the other children butchered in front of her before escaping. Now she was haunted with the memory and terrified of anyone who approached her.*

*At the end of our visit to Rwanda, and the Zairean refugee camps, we went to Goma to meet up with a Swiss colleague to compare notes and plan together. The following day we woke up to a real disaster. The town of 120,000 people had, overnight, increased its population to over a million. The scene was indescribable. Seas of refugees were pouring into Goma at an estimated 50,000 an hour! In the streets there was no room for cars – just thousands and thousands of people, all carrying what they could salvage from their homes, some with sheep and cattle, many dragging desperately tired and foot-sore children.*

*The relief agencies already in Goma worked closely together to try to meet some of the needs of the refugees. Each night there was an emergency co-ordination meeting, at which we were briefed of the current situation. As we drove home after the meeting, the crowds of people became a blanket of bodies covering every available space in the town. Each night as I went to bed, I felt I was lying among those sleeping bodies. Each morning, as the crowds moved on towards the refugee camps, they left behind those who did not wake up. Thousands and thousands have died, and are dying still. Bodies are wrapped up and left by the roadside for collection and burial in the mass graves.*

*A couple of days after the arrival of the first wave of refugees, fighting broke out in the border town of Gisenyi (Rwanda), less than a mile from where we were in Goma (Zaïre). The airport at Goma was shelled, and many died in a rocket attack at the border post. We took a child from the arms of his dead mother. The Archdeacon of Goma's wife cared for him for the night, but she already had several thousands of people on her doorstep. The following day we took the child to one of the orphanages. There are now over 6,000 such orphans or lost children! The fighting continued for several days and nights, and it was impossible to sleep.*

*About five days later, the cholera epidemic broke out and spread like a forest fire. Our mission changed. Immediately we were immersed in emergency relief work, supporting local churches as they tried to cope with an impossible situation. In each small church compound there were up to 5,000 people camping. Toilet facilities were non-existent! Goma is built on volcanic larva so it is virtually impossible to dig holes in the ground, water was unavailable. There was no food, and health centres could not cope. A journalist described the situation as 'an unimaginable sight of sheer hell'. Oxfam, Médicins Sans Frontiers, UN agencies, the International Red Cross and others worked together in establishing supplies. However, the response from Europe and America was pathetic, and we all knew that we were fighting a losing battle. I radioed to Nyankunde to ask my colleagues to send five nurses down immediately. They arrived in an MAF plane the following day. They were stunned by the sight which met them, and by the very poor conditions in which all of us were living, but have since worked hard in one church compound where there are over 300 new cases of cholera a day. In all, between the various Protestant churches with which we are working, we have about 1,500 new cases a day. The death rate is very high, and during the day the bodies pile up beside the camps. Nyankunde Hospital is now making intravenous fluids round the clock for us, and MAF is flying them down to Goma. I have never in my life worked in such circumstances, and pray that such a disaster will never again hit the world.*

*I am actually writing this from a beautiful spot, not far from Nyankunde. It is a different world from the horrors of Goma! Together with other Professors of Community Health, I have been sharing in a workshop to plan the new course at Nyankunde which opens in October: a Bachelor's degree in community health – the first in Zaïre. I am head of the department of community health, and so was obliged to attend. In fact it has been four days of bliss (hot showers, clean fresh air, good food, water to drink, and nights free from gun-fire) and I feel ready to return to Goma tomorrow.*

## LL70: December 1994

*The situation in Goma remains very tense, still with over a million refugees in the camps. Although food, water and medical supplies are now fairly well organised, camps breed insecurity and tension. The largest camp has over 300,000 people, all living in extraordinarily cramped conditions. Recently a refugee asked me how she could learn to cope with living in such close proximity to her neighbours, and be able to get along with them! Having had 20 refugees in my home for six weeks, I could understand what she was saying, but the camp situation is so extreme that I had no words of wisdom or advice to offer.*

*Let me give you a few glimpses of camp life:*

- *A widow with her malnourished child does not have the strength to stand in the queue for her food rations. She asks a neighbour to help, but the neighbour runs off with her double helping.*
- *A teenager helps her sick mother along the road, but the mother dies on the way to get help. The child has no strength to dig a hole to bury her mother. She wraps a cloth around the body, and walks on, leaving her mother's body to be collected later by the camp scouts.*

- *A young man who had done well in business, but who now has nothing, climbs a hill in Goma (Zaïre), and looks over to his own house in Gisenyi (Rwanda). He cannot go back because he fears for his life. He can see that his house has become 'possessed' by newly returned Rwandans (possibly those who have been in Uganda for a generation). He returns to his plastic shelter feeling utterly defeated.*
- *A young family decides to return to Rwanda, since their fate there, they suppose, cannot be worse than in the camps. They climb on the top of a pick-up truck – but are suddenly beaten off – and are later found dead.*

The stories go on . . . but there are good things too. Walking around the camps, one can see amazing initiatives. UNICEF biscuit tins are beaten into pots and pans; UNHCR plastic sheeting is cut up in attractive designs and fringes to decorate a tent-bar/hotel; primary school children gather on the side of a road with a teacher and recite their lessons (of course, no materials, benches etc., but the volcanic ash on the road is useful for making designs or writing out tests!); some people have used pieces of larval rock to construct low walls around their plastic sheeting, making a hermit's cave among the pandemonium of the camp. On a Sunday morning, as one walks through the camps, every half-kilometre or so there is a camp church – no buildings or plastic sheeting, but pieces of larval rock put in rows. An Anglican liturgy in Kinurwanda (or any other pattern of service) may be intensely conservative, but praising, worshipping and praying for daily needs in that situation is so real that one senses a nearness to heaven which is seldom present in the most elaborate or modern churches. One has a similar feeling when saying grace before sharing a few beans and maize: 'Help us to be grateful, and to help those who have less than we do . . .' One might expect that people who have so suffered might turn against God and the church, but the hope of even the most marginalised is amazing. Maybe our social security deprives us of gratitude and hope!

In Rwanda the situation is very different from the camps in Zaïre. One feels much more secure, and is aware of commodities coming back into the shops. Telecommunications, power and water are available (seldom or never available in Zaïre!), and people are trying to live a normal life, or to restore their former homes and lives. However, instead of French being used everywhere, English has become very important, *with long-term refugees returning from Tanzania, Uganda and European countries where they have been in exile for a generation or more. I visited friends in Kigali, who had been among the refugees in my home in May/June. They had lost everything, and their home had been badly damaged, but they were grateful to have a house rather than a tent.*

*We have just completed training for 'camp facilitators' – refugees who will promote community initiatives, and assist the neglected camp members. I am increasingly humbled by the capacity of those who have suffered so much, and I have come away feeling I have gained much more from their stamina than they have gained from my simple teaching.*

*There are a great number of aid organisations in all the refugee areas and in Rwanda, and considerable collaboration between them, with valiant overall co-ordination by the United Nations High Commission for Refugees (UNHCR). Not least in all this activity has been the role played by the local Zairean churches, in the support and help they have given to the refugees, often at considerable cost to themselves.*

*Our seventh course has just finished; our classroom block is completed; our 'Chichester Diocese' vehicle is proving its worth; the cows, goats and rabbits are increasing; the fields have had a good harvest and Kaswera and Kaluma have completed their Master's degrees in Liverpool and return in January. The university-level nurses' training has begun at the* Institut Supérieur des Techniques Médicales *(ISTM), where I am Head of the Department of Community Health. ISTM and IPASC are very close, but my priorities rest with the IPASC team. Next week I will be in Guinea (Conakry) helping Protestant medical health groups to form a co-ordinating agency, and then I will have two weeks in England before returning to Nyankunde and Goma.*

*The reason for my journey to Bukavu this weekend is to work with the Norwegian Church Aid team in the Rwandan refugee camps. Earlier this year all of us involved in the work of refugees (the ACIST programme which is co-ordinated by the World Council of Churches), met in Mokono, Uganda, to review the progress made in Tanzania, Burundi, Rwanda and Zaïre. On the way home one of the vehicles crashed, killing a Norwegian colleague. In Bukavu I will be spending time with those who were also involved in the accident. At the same time, together with a German colleague, I will be finishing off a comprehensive evaluation of the nursing school supported by Tearfund.*

*My visit to the camps was interesting. The situation in Bukavu is very different from that of the camps in Goma. In Bukavu there are 300,000 refugees divided between 32 camps. There is enough room between tents for the refugees to have one metre of garden around the tent, thus providing vegetables to improve their monotonous rations. There are many social activities, so few people stay in the tent doing nothing. Goma, by contrast, has over a million refugees, divided between about four camps (the largest camp has 300,000 people). The tents are pitched on larval rock and are tightly packed together, allowing no privacy. There are no gardens, and life is tough. In both Goma and Bukavu our teams are supporting social groups among the refugees. There are orphans making cakes, widows knitting and sewing, youth groups making children's toys, and a growing number of camp churches and libraries. Between our various teams we must have about 200 small-group activities. The teams in Rwanda have similar activities, but they can build more specifically for the future. While I was in Bukavu, we heard that our Rwandan team witnessed the aftermath of the massacre in south western Rwanda (over 2,000 killed in a camp). This news made the situation in Bukavu tense.*

### LL76: December 1996

*The situation here in Zaïre is changing very rapidly. Towards the end of October (1996), so-called 'rebel' forces (combined opposition groups) infiltrated the Great Lakes area of Zaïre (the area to the west of Lakes Tanganyika and Kivu), and moved northwards to Goma. For the past two years this area has been the home of over a million Rwandan refugees living in huge camps – hostages of their own militia. The unexpected incursions threw the region into chaos. The local Zairean military forces, unpaid for years, took advantage of the insecurity and began rampant looting, rape and abuse. Meanwhile, the Rwandan militia dispersed into the hills, leaving the refugees to escape. About half of them returned to Rwanda, while the other half fled west into the forests and harsh terrain.*

*How did all these movements affect the church? Several major Christian hospitals were attacked by the military, in some instances with patients and staff killed, and in all cases with severe looting. The immediate consequences of the fighting were reduced food and cash availability, and so Zaireans ran in any direction which they consid-*

*ered relatively safe and where they might find food. Many pastors went to the Bishop's compound in Bukavu, where some Rwandan refugees remained. The Bishop found himself feeding hundreds of people, trusting on the goodwill from partners overseas to help him meet the bill. Archdeacon Masimango (Bishop-elect of Kindu) had been due to leave for Kindu to prepare for his consecration – planned for January. He was stuck in Goma, where, once he had recovered from several days of existing without food, he headed up an ecumenical team to cope with internally displaced Zairean persons ('IDPs' is the official term) who had fled from the town during the fighting and returned to find homes and possessions gone.*

*Tearfund quickly responded to some of Masimango's needs. Dr Jo Lusi, a surgeon friend of ours, found his team at the Baptist Hospital in Goma dwindled to almost nothing as frightened staff abandoned their posts. Left with no food, no fuel and few staff, he battled on with war injuries, cholera and illnesses resulting from deprivation. The hospital was running at three times its capacity. At one point Jo ordered that the doors of the operating room be broken down and the wood used for fuel to sterilise his surgical equipment. While the needs of that hospital are being met through international Christian organisations, and taken in by his wife, Lyn, who is based in Nairobi, Jo has not had a break for six weeks.*

*Further west, a large group of refugees (about 500,000) was wandering aimlessly – not knowing the routes or the terrain, and exhausted by heat, rain, illness and hunger. While international agencies discussed the disappearance of these refugees, and the possibility of their never having existed, we monitored their movements and tried to get help to them. At one moment I heard on the BBC that planes were flying over the area to map the groups of refugees – and at the same time, on our inter-mission radio, colleagues were telling us that the refugees were fleeing into the bush at the sound of circling aircraft! No wonder the mappers could not see them! On another occasion I heard a reporter on the BBC say that the aid agencies were 'making up the story of refugees so that it would make a good story for their Christmas Appeals'! That hurt! Praise God that organisations such as Tearfund and Christian Aid are telling the truth, and getting information from those of us who were on the spot and knew what was happening.*

*We were able to work closely with Tearfund, and were delighted when several plane loads of medicines arrived for the refugees. Sadly the logistics of getting them south to where the refugees and IDPs were proved much more difficult. Christian organisations, however, do not always get the protocol right. One such organisation (not one that would be known to most folk in the UK) was less than sensitive in coming into Nyankunde, via Bunia, with a plane load of medicine but without having the necessary permission. The people on the plane had got hold of my name and used it as a reference – which led to my being held and interrogated for two days: not a pleasant experience!*

*As the 'rebels' pushed northwards, the Zairean military retreated before them with their terrorising looting and abuse. Wave after wave of these retreating soldiers arrived at Bunia, often passing through Nyankunde. For me the experience was at the same time terrifying and reassuring: terrifying as I became decreasingly resistant to the sight and sound of soldiers and guns; reassuring as time and again we were protected from harm despite some very dramatic incidents. At one time about ten senior staff members and pilots were together in the hangar of the Mission Aviation Fellowship (MAF). A local soldier, threatened and frightened by a retreating militia group, lost his head and started firing. After an hour or so of shooting and hysterical behaviour the only damage was a crate full of broken bottles and a damaged electrical system where bullets had cut through wiring – and one minor gun-powder wound.*

*However, while we were protected, many folk have suffered. One of the worst fears was that of rape. Girls were hidden in bushes, or sent away into the countryside to protect them from the soldiers. On one occasion a stolen tractor passed through Nyankunde with young girls from another town tied on and held at gunpoint. They cried to us for help – and we could only look on with impotence.*

*By the end of the first week of November, teaching had become increasingly difficult. Most of my time was spent monitoring the refugee and IDP (internally displaced persons) movements, and liaising with outside organisations in the attempt to get help. Other staff played volleyball with the students or made their lessons very practical. Often I would sit with the students in the evening, in an attempt to calm them (and perhaps to calm myself!). David Moore (a volunteer from Liverpool) and Graham Gordon (Tearfund) had to evacuate to another station for one weekend, but I was glad that they returned before the other evacuees as both have been a tremendous support in keeping things going. Eventually Graham went to Uganda to look at the possibility of evacuating IPASC there. The Ugandan Government would not accept Zairean nationals, but at least it was a relief to evacuate our non-Zairean students to Uganda. They were destined for Kiwoko Hospital, but, en route, spent five nights in Entebbe Airport (with Graham) before the Immigration Authorities would allow them in. At this point we were most grateful to CMS and Church of Uganda colleagues who went out of their way to help with the necessary paperwork.*

*Throughout all the tensions, the inter-mission collaboration was superb. Local Christians and expatriate personnel worked together to sustain communications, and to inform one another of impending dangers. After the evacuation of mission partners from Boga, Nyangoma Kabarole and her brothers assumed a very important role in the network, and it was they who finally warned us that we should evacuate. The last pilots and I left for Entebbe in Uganda on Monday 2 December after more drama at Nyankunde, and with fighting on both sides of the town.*

*Flying out of the situation was an enormous relief. I had reached the point where I had no courage left. I was angry at the unnecessary damage and hurt to the local folk, and disappointed that, with all the information we had about refugees and IDPs, we could not reach them with the medical resources we had already received from Tearfund and Norwegian Church Aid.*

*I was powerless to lead my own team, as I was flying out on the only remaining plane – which, the day before, we had planned to hire in order to move the remaining staff and students further away from the fighting. I felt that I was absconding, running away, leaving my friends to cope. All these feelings were similar to those felt by other CMS mission partners. How good that CMS' experience meant that the folk in London could anticipate our needs, and that Peter Kenworthy (Personnel Manager) and Chris Carey (Regional Secretary for East and Central Africa) flew to Kampala to meet with us and to debrief before we thought about the next step. This very sensitive action prevented some of the distress of leaving Zaïre, since we were quickly able to see things in the right perspective.*

*I am home for a two-week break, having left Graham Gordon and Dr Elsbeth Schmid with our non-Zairean students at Kiwoko Hospital, north of Kampala. On 21 December I will be heading back to Uganda to join the 'IPASCians-in-exile' for Christmas. By the beginning of January some major decisions will have to be made concerning the future of the school. With all the senior staff and advisers of IPASC still in Zaïre, and out of communication, this is going to be a difficult exercise – so I will appreciate your prayers for wisdom.*

## IPASC evacuates foreign staff and students: 15 December 1996

*Towards the end of October, so-called 'rebel' forces (combined opposition groups) infiltrated the Great Lakes area of Zaïre (the area to the west of Lakes Tanganyika and Kivu), and moved northwards to Goma. For the past two years this area has been the home of over a million Rwandan refugees living in huge camps – hostages of their own militia. The unexpected incursions threw the region into chaos. The local Zairean military forces, unpaid for years, took advantage of the insecurity and began rampant looting, rape and abuse. Meanwhile, the Rwandan militia dispersed into the hills, leaving the refugees to escape. About half of them returned to Rwanda, while the other half fled west into the forests and harsh terrain.*

*Several major hospitals were attacked by the military, in some instances with patients and staff killed, and in all cases with severe looting. The immediate consequences of the fighting were reduced food and cash availability, and so Zaireans ran in any direction which they considered relatively safe and where they might find food. Dr Jo Lusi, a surgeon and one of IPASC's founding members, found his team at the Baptist Hospital in Goma dwindled to almost nothing as frightened staff abandoned their posts. Left with no food, no fuel and few staff, he battled on with war injuries, cholera and illnesses of deprivation. The hospital was running at three times its capacity. At one point Jo ordered that the doors of the operating room be broken down and the wood used for fuel to sterilise his surgical equipment.*

*Further west, a large group of refugees (about 500,000) was wandering aimlessly – not knowing the routes or the terrain, and exhausted by heat, rain, illness and hunger. While international agencies discussed the disappearance of these refugees, and the possibility of their never having existed, we, at IPASC, much further north in Nyankunde, monitored their movements and tried to get help to them. We were able to work closely with Tearfund, and were delighted when several planeloads of medicines arrived for the refugees. Sadly, the logistics of getting them south to where the refugees and internally displaced persons*

*(IDPs) were, proved much more difficult. Relief agencies, however, do not always get the protocol right. One such agency was less than sensitive in coming into Nyankunde, via Bunia, with a planeload of medicines, but without having the necessary permission. The people on the plane had got hold of my name, and used it as a reference – which led to my being held and interrogated for two days by the authorities. This was a terrifying experience, as bullets were flying, and I was alone in a melee of madness, oiled by drunkenness. I had organised a Tearfund flight, but had kept to the rules. Having my passport confiscated, being kept in isolation, and being classed as a traitor was one of the most frightening experiences I had ever had. On top of this, to be apparently a traitor, who had done everything wrong, when I had done everything right, felt awful when I always taught that we have to conform to authorities, whatever we feel about them.*

*I felt lonely – with my own home only half a mile away down the airstrip and all my friends there. They did not know why I was being held. Eventually, the immigration authorities decided to take me to Bunia. With me was an American doctor and his colleague who had brought in a plane illegally, and who, not knowing the area or the authorities, was behaving very arrogantly and foolishly, even as he was being mishandled and put back on the plane for which he was responsible. He refused to fly with guns put in the 'pod' of the plane. At that point, the situation was so volatile that any argument was foolish. As I, like a lamb led to the slaughter, did as I was told, and went towards the plane, Tony Ukety, the Medical Director and one of IPASC's founding members, came to see what was happening. He asked the authorities why I was being taken as a prisoner. Diplomatically, he said that he was responsible for me, and so anything for which I had to answer, he could answer for me. He suggested that, because I was only a woman (but a woman who had lived there for many years), I should not be questioned, but that he would take my place. What a Christian move – taking my place. Clearly Tony knew how to play the game, but it could have gone in any direction, probably subject to the amount of alcohol that had been consumed. My passport was thrown back at me, and Tony got in the plane. The arrogant doctor who had caused all the pain left even more arrogant and foolish. Apparently, at Bunia airport, the doctor was deported and banned from coming back to Zaïre. Tony walked away from the situation. As he suspected, they would have let me go in Bunia. It was just beyond their pride to admit that they had made a serious mistake at Nyankunde. But what a very frightening experience!*

*As the plane took off at Nyankunde, I walked down the airstrip to IPASC thinking that my colleagues would come running up to welcome me. But there was nothing and I remained lonely and lost. Where was everyone? On the IPASC compound, a few colleagues came up to me, and I wanted to tell them everything in one breath – but they were telling me everything in one breath. When the gunfire started and they knew I was in the middle of it, the driver ran back down to the IPASC compound, telling everyone that I had been abducted. Quickly the staff hid the radio, as they guessed that the military authorities would look for a radio to use, and they knew that the military authorities were not to be trusted. Then the Chief, who had heard that I was in the middle of the gunfire, wanted to send an urgent message to the authorities in Bunia to protect me. So he came to IPASC to use our radio. By then, to protect the radio from the military, the radio had been buried, but the staff who had buried it had gone back to the village, and those who were around did not know where it had been buried. They found it, but could not tell the Chief it was buried, so put me with the Chief to 'chat' while they dug it up. I could not work out what was going on, and why they were not jumping with delight that I was free. Instead there was a cup of tea between me and the Chief and a silent conversation, neither of us knowing the other's thoughts! Eventually, one of my colleagues called me to the radio – which looked very normal – but I did not know of its 'journey' over the past hours! They said in a loud, and very polite voice, 'It's OK for the Chief to use the radio to call the authorities in Bunia isn't it?' Bizarre! Why ask me? With my back to the Chief, I looked quizzically at the enquirer. 'Fine' he said, without waiting for a reply, but setting the radio up for the Chief. They led me out, and collapsed in laughter, while I collapsed in the pain of trauma, the details of which colleagues had no idea. We went over to my house, where there was a real cup of tea and welcome, leaving someone to take care of the Chief. They listened with concern and pain at all that had happened once the driver had left me at the hangar. We prayed together, but, for me, the pain lasted for a long time, and I was left shaken by the horrid incident.*

*As the 'rebels' (nothing to do with local rebels) pushed northwards from Goma, the Zairean military preceded them with their terrorising, looting, rape and abuse. Wave after wave of these retreating soldiers arrived at Bunia, often passing through Nyankunde. I became decreasingly resistant to the sight and sound of soldiers and guns, though we were protected from harm despite some very dramatic incidents. On one occasion about ten senior staff members and pilots were together in the hangar of the Mission Aviation Fellowship (MAF). A local soldier, threatened and frightened by a retreating militia group, lost his head and started firing. After an hour or so of shooting and hysterical behaviour the only damage was a crate full of broken bottles and a damaged electrical system where bullets had cut through wiring – and one minor gunpowder wound. However, while we were protected, many folk have suffered. One of the worst fears was that of rape. Girls were hidden in bushes, or sent away into the countryside to protect them from the soldiers. A stolen tractor passed through Nyankunde with young girls from another town tied on and held at gunpoint. They cried to us for help – and we could only look on with impotence.*

*By the end of the first week of November, teaching at IPASC had become increasingly difficult. Most of my time was spent monitoring the refugee and IDP movements, and liaising with outside organisations in the attempt to get help. Eventually we looked at the possibility of evacuating IPASC to Uganda. The Ugandan Government would not accept Zairean nationals, but at least it was a relief to send our non-Zairean students out of Zaïre. They were destined for Kiwoko Hospital, but en route spent five nights in Entebbe Airport before the Immigration authorities would allow them in. At this point we were most grateful to colleagues who went out of their way to help with the necessary paperwork.*

*Local friends and expatriate personnel worked together in Zaïre to sustain communications, and to inform one another of impending dangers. The last pilots and I left for Entebbe in Uganda on Monday 2 December after more drama at Nyankunde, and with fighting on both sides of the town. Flying out of the situation was an enormous relief. I had reached the point where I had no courage left. I was angry at the unnecessary damage and hurt to the local folk, and disappointed that, with all the information we had about refugees and IDPs, we could not reach them with the medical resources we had already received. I was powerless to lead my own team, as I was flying out on the only remaining plane – which, the day before, we had planned to hire in order to move the remaining staff and students further away from the fighting. I felt that I was absconding; running away; leaving my friends to cope.*

*Inevitably, our letters tell the stories from our point of view, and leave out some of the key actors. While we have the privilege of being able to get things back into perspective in comfort (albeit in the cold of a British winter), our national colleagues continue to work in the very difficult situation from which we evacuated. The courage of people like Nyangoma Kabarole and her brothers Kagwa and Kabeba (beaten by retreating troops as they looted Boga earlier this week); of Dr Jo Lusi in Goma, and Dr Tony Ukety at Nyankunde, far exceeded and continues to exceed anything that we tried to do.*

*It has been good to keep in touch with LSTM during this difficult period, and we have been grateful for your messages and encourage- ment. By the beginning of January some major decisions will have to be made concerning the future of the school. With all the senior staff and advisers of IPASC still in Zaïre, and out of communication, this is going to be a difficult exercise.*

*Evacuating from Nyankunde to Kiwoko Hospital in Uganda with our non-Zairean students before Christmas provided an unexpected, but pleasant, temporary home. However, the journey was dramatic. Although we were able to get the necessary travel and immigration documents, the challenge of having so many people from different countries, travelling via NE DR Congo, left authorities puzzled. The students were not allowed out of the transit lounge of the airport, while the Europeans were not allowed to stay in the transit lounge. However, through the British Embassy, foreign staff were eventually able to teach the students in the lounge, causing much fascination for cleaners and those staffing the restaurant. I came onto the scene several days later, and it was good to make friends with various people around the airport. Nevertheless, the situation was bizarre and we needed help. It was the Archbishop of Uganda who appealed to the President of Uganda, and the whole situation was resolved very easily. In fact, the President insisted that the students be given a visa for six months, allowing each student the freedom of the country during that time.*

*The Church of Uganda Hospital at Kiwoko responded generously to our cry for help, handing over to us a recently built training centre and dormitories. Kiwoko itself is a very busy hospital, but the staff went out of their way to make us welcome and to provide accommo- dation for us, i.e. three staff members (from England and Switzerland) and eleven students (from Bénin, Cameroun, Tchad, Burundi, Angola and Central African Republic). Our main objective was to complete the semester for the non-Zairean students, so that they would not lose this academic year. By the first week of January we were able to arrange flights for these students and send them to their own countries for their practical periods. Dr Elsbeth Schmid did most of the teaching, while Graham Gordon (a Tearfund gap-year) very capably handled the administration and the finance. I was so grateful to both of them. Elsbeth is now working in Tchad and Graham is awaiting possible relocation.*

*Once the students were on their way home, I went to Nairobi where I stayed with Masumbuku and his family. He is the treasurer at the hospital at Nyankunde, and, being the only person with the key to the cash box, was at considerable risk while he stayed in Zaïre. Several senior staff members and their families walked for several days until they reached Uganda. These included Masumbuku and Dr Ukety, the district medical officer who had been badly beaten. They found public transport in Uganda and eventually made their way to Nairobi, Kenya.*

*During January, we tried to work out a communication system with our colleagues in Zaïre. At least this helped us to catch little bits of news, and from this communication we knew that the Nyankunde folk were very short of food and cash, but that things were relatively calm. Our remaining students had been sent to Boga. Most of the staff remained at Nyankunde, but we cannot imagine the real situation in which they were living.*

*We have learned, with great sadness, of the death of some of our friends – several nurses, two of our drivers, a pastor and his family, and a few less well-known Nyankunde folk. Further south some clergy have also been killed. All were shot by retreating military forces, some while running from their homes which had been set on fire. Boga also had a very bad time, and Nyangoma's brothers were badly beaten. Nevertheless, very recent news from Boga assures us that Nyangoma is well, though tired. She and her brothers and other team members are tremendously courageous and faithful.*

*It is too early to count all the damage that has been done. Boga lost a great deal, as did Nyankunde and Bunia. My house was broken into (apparently soldiers were looking for arms!), but I had little of value to be stolen (books, papers and clothes). Fortunately we had sent all our important documents, and the back-up disks of all our computer documents, out of the country.*

*Many mission partners have had their homes looted.*

## LL77: *February 1997*

*Being in Cape Town gave me the opportunity to meet up with a pilot and his wife, who had arrived in Nyankunde at the end of October (1996). Their story may help you to pray for some of the mission families. Tanya and John Boyd were married five years ago. Soon after their wedding they applied to the Mission Aviation Fellowship. They spent the following four years preparing for missionary service in the United States – flying training, Bible school and language study. Eventually, when they arrived at Nyankunde with their young son Stewart, they started to set up the first real home they have had and began to unpack their wedding presents. Only thirteen days later, following the first shooting incident at Nyankunde, they were evacuated at fifteen minutes' notice (and so they had no time to pack). Two weeks later, everything in their home was looted. Four years preparation; thirteen days at Nyankunde, and they have lost everything except Stewart and their lovely two-week-old daughter! This week they will be relocated. Pray for mission-partner families.*

*Seeing John Boyd was special for me, because he was my partner (as logistics officer) when we were monitoring the half a million refugees in October and November (1996). We were together in one of the shooting incidents, and I found it healing to recall the events of that day together, with Tanya adding pieces to the jigsaw. John had been able to escape halfway through the incident (he had been outside the hangar, whereas the rest of us were inside), and had carefully kept a check on the timing of activities. Interestingly, I had totally underestimated the time and severity of the situation. While I was talking about a one-hour episode, he confirmed that we were held in the hangar by the gunman for three hours. I said that only a few rounds of ammunition were fired (twelve) but he counted over 30! How useful amnesia is!*

*I don't think I would like to have known the truth any earlier, but now I understand why my colleagues and students at IPASC were so concerned for me. Moving about so much over the past two months has meant that Christmas has been prolonged, and I have enjoyed receiving Christmas cards at each of my stops: some arrived in Zaïre before I evacuated during the first week of December, others in Uganda, Kenya, England and South Africa. I have appreciated each one so much, and many of you have written very sensitively as you have* shared some of the pain of the situation in Zaïre. Thank you very much for your expressions of love and concern.

### LL78: 18 May 1997

*I am sure that many of you will have been following the news from Zaïre over the weekend of 17–18 May. I was eagerly watching TV in Nairobi as Laurent Kabila and the 'rebels' approached and eventually took Kinshasa, the capital city.*

*I tried to watch with the eyes of a British person, sitting in an armchair in England. The people looked very poor; their treatment of one another was rough; laughter and singing punctuated the loud grieving over the dead and dying; the only paid soldiers in the country (the Presidential Guard) surrendered to rebel teenage soldiers; and the general population vacillated between a confidence in Kabila and fear that one dictatorship would replace another.*

*Meanwhile negotiations, on a South African frigate off the coast of Zaïre and in Gabon, led foreign powers to hope for a peaceful outcome. The negotiations changed nothing, least of all Mr Kabila's determination to march into Kinshasa and take the city and the country. As with all the cities in Zaïre, force was hardly necessary, as Government troops surrendered, knowing the inevitable consequences of a battle. Mr Mobutu similarly capitulated, and slid out of the country into exile. How are the mighty fallen! In seven months, Kabila and his alliance progressed from an apparently insignificant uprising in south eastern Zaïre to becoming the leaders of the Democratic Republic of Congo (the new name for Zaïre). In contrast, Mr Mobutu – one of the richest men in the world (who has led one of the poorest countries for over 30 years, stealing its mineral wealth) and now weakened by cancer – has been humiliated and defeated.*

*So what is the future for IPASC; for the Diocese of Boga and for the remaining refugees in the middle of the country? IPASC lost six weeks of term during the fighting and insecurity at Nyankunde, which was severe and terrifying. Since then, the staff and students have resumed activities, and have saved the academic year. We have yet to bring back our foreign students who are presently in their own countries. The courage and ability of my colleagues has been amazing, and I praise God for their confidence and perseverance. One of our most important immediate jobs will be to introduce ourselves to the new government officials and to be part of the building of a new health infrastructure.*

*For the Diocese of Boga there will be new opportunities – but much re-building of lives, property and confidence will be needed. At Boga, Nyangoma has held the health service together, but badly needs a rest. For the refugees, the future is less certain and not at all bright. Hundreds of thousands fled over 1,000km across very inhospitable country into the forest of central Zaïre.*

*Repatriation to Rwanda is complicated and expensive and does not guarantee them a safe life ahead. Their physical and mental trauma leaves them as victims of an unbelievable hostage crisis where most were held as human shields for the few escaping from retribution, following the Rwanda genocide of 1994.*

*The Archbishop (Njojo) has invited mission partners to return, and CMS has agreed. There are very few expatriates in the country now, and most other missionary societies have decided to wait before return-ing, since there are very few communications, or support systems. Much has been looted or destroyed and there is still only a fragile sense of security.*

*I am writing this, having just returned from a Communion service at Nairobi Cathedral this Pentecost Sunday. The Revd Andy Wheeler, a CMS colleague, was the preacher. Andy always gives himself com-pletely in his ministry, but this time he was particularly challenging. His theme was: 'The living God wants to have a deep, transforming relationship with you and me'.*

*As we concentrated on the power of the Holy Spirit in transforming lives, on renewal and resurrection joy, and on a commitment to peace and justice, I thought of the mission ahead of me . . . Tomorrow I return – not to Zaïre, but to the Democratic Republic of Congo (Kabila changed the name back to its original name, as he took over power); not to war, but to reconstruction; not to the same team, but to a team which, in my absence, has already had a transforming experience; not to the familiar village and friends, but to the charred remains of homes, and to the widows and bereaved children of friends; not to e-mail and easy communications, but to relative isolation. I feel renewed and ready, blessed and commissioned, but need to maintain an acceptance of God's 'transforming relationship'. Pray that the Holy Spirit will equip me for all that is ahead, and equip us all to take our part in rebuilding a country and a church with a huge potential.*

### LL79: 13 July 1997

*What's in a name? I left Zaïre in December, and returned on the day that the Democratic Republic of Congo was born in May. A new country which has inherited old problems . . . and superimposed upon the old problems are those related to the devastation caused by the war.*

*The scars of war are all around us, and much of everyday conversations, church sermons and prayers relate to the various experiences of the war. For the past few months, we have been 'mopping up'. This has included visiting the bereaved and those who lost their homes (133 homes were burned); patching up our own homes and replacing looted necessary goods; re-establishing a routine and psychologically adjusting to the new situation.*

*Yesterday all the institutions at Nyankunde (the nursing school, the university, IPASC, the Mission Aviation Fellowship, the deaf school, the church, the hospital, etc.) joined together for a day of thanksgiving for deliverance from the old regime and from the war. It was a happy day of worship, fun and sports. Now we need to look ahead, get on with life, and help to rebuild the country. For most of us, this is a challenge that, despite the ongoing difficulties, we are ready to meet. But for many others, there are enormous barriers to overcome.*

*There are still well over 100,000 Rwandan refugees in the country. Dr François Mwema, one of my colleagues, spent December to June in the camps around Kisangani. He returned to Nyankunde in the middle of June, and the following day he and I headed south to Goma and Bukavu to evaluate an Oxfam water and sanitation programme. During the following two weeks we experienced the insecurity of these areas, but then the British medical emergency programme MERLIN pleaded with us to give them a hand. Refugees coming out of the forest several hundred kilometres west of Bukavu were in a very poor condition. Many were being brought to a hospital with an exceptionally high mortality rate.*

*The situation was so bad that we had to take radical action. François took over the hospital, while I established a public health and immunisation programme. The hospital was part of the government structure – but where was the Government? We worked with the United Nations High Commission for Refugees (UNHCR), CARE International, and Oxfam, as well as with the MERLIN team, to bring about some order. The sights, the sounds and the stories were* horrific. How can these devastated people meet the 'challenge' of a new life (in Rwanda)? Maybe one poor mother demonstrated the easiest way out. Her nine children and her husband died in the forest, and she was left with an eighteen-month-old weighing 4kg – who was determined to live. Not so the mother. She could not cope with her memories, and, despite the care given, was determined to die. She left behind her orphan, who was picked up by another refugee mother.

The challenges we face are going to take a long time to work through. Communications are very difficult at present. We seldom have planes in from Nairobi so most of our correspondence is done by radio e-mail, which is working fairly well again (thanks to MAF). Local flying is limited, though we will have two planes and two pilots here by the end of next week (MAF lost most of their property during the war). We have electricity very rarely and some days there is no water available. Food is scarce and prices are high because of the drought. Emotions are fragile as people nurse their traumatic experiences and hurts.

I thank God for an excellent team at IPASC. The staff have not only coped with the emergency but have also developed their respective areas of work. The community health school is going well under Katembo Kaluma's direction; Kaswera's Safe Motherhood programme is exciting and Paluku Sabuni, just back from completing his Master's degree at Liverpool, has taken on the huge task of supporting health services, for which he has master-minded a superb programme.

François, with his wife Pitchu and their four daughters, need time to settle down after the nightmares of living in Kisangani during the war, but it already feels very good to have them back. They add maturity and a special spiritual dimension to the team.

Our immediate plans will take Sabuni and myself north of Kisangani (central-northern Congo) to visit the health programmes of the Norwegian Baptist Church, for whom we are technical advisers. The folk there have had most of their property looted, and we need to help them know what is left and what needs to be done first. We are just waiting for the folk there to cut the respective air-strips (which usually takes a couple of weeks using hand scythes). In August we have our three-yearly external evaluation, our annual audit and then our Administrative Council. In September I will be teaching in Liverpool before beginning the new academic year here in October.

Nearer to home is Marabo village, just four kilometres from Nyankunde. Our students were doing some field work at Marabo a couple of weeks ago. When Paluku Sabuni (the lecturer in charge of health services) and I looked at the results, we could not believe them – the students recorded a 50% malnutrition rate, with many of those children being very severely malnourished. Sabuni and I went up to check. To our horror, the results were correct. We found a community of several thousand in a desperate situation – right on our doorstep! The village was always poor, but the war and the recent drought (which continues) have pushed them over the poverty cliff into the pit of destitution. Once in that pit, people lose hope easily.

Since then one or other member of staff has visited daily. Sabuni has developed an excellent relationship with the people and won their confidence – but where do we start? Kaswera Vulere (in charge of our Family Health and Safe Motherhood programme), sensing their hopelessness, asked the women if they would like her to pray with them. Several broke down and sobbed. They were experiencing love and concern for the first time in months, and their tears were simply a release of fear and an expression of new hope.

François and I went up to the village today to take some fish and eggs to one little seven-year-old girl named Mandeke (her name means 'born on the road-side'). Her grandmother is her guardian, and we know that there is no way she would take Mandeke to hospital, even though she may well die at home. There are so many others to care for, and anyway, where would she get the money from to pay for the care? Sabuni is juggling with the problem of how to respond to the emergency and, at the same time, to the development needs of the village. Charity will get them nowhere, but lack of it will only leave them in their pit of despair, from where they cannot even face the challenges of a new country.

Even when one thinks that problems are over, new problems quickly appear. Boga was ahead of Nyankunde in its rehabilitation when, about a month ago, troubles across the border in Uganda brought over a thousand refugees into the Boga area. It feels like one step forward and two steps back; but, I think, on the whole, it is rather two steps forward and an occasional one backwards.

## LL81: 14 September 1998

*The kaleidoscope cannot handle the scenes of my evacuation from the Congo, and I do not want to recall them. The process was horrid as numerous border officials poured verbal abuse, intimidation and delaying tactics on those of us trying to leave the country. The procedure took two days. But this was relatively simple. Louise Wright and Emma Wild (both of CMS), with three American colleagues, spent three weeks trying to leave Kindu. The MAF pilot who had gone to pick them up was also kept at Kindu and not allowed access to his plane. All are out now, and no one has come to any real harm.*

*The next and last scene is a painful one. I know that, at present, my colleagues in Nyankunde are in hiding in the bush, and I have been able to contact them by satellite telephone. They are safe, but the situation is precarious. Cholera is proving a constant hazard for those living in villages with unprotected water supplies, and there is a meningitis epidemic.*

*I have been thinking of my neighbours at Nyankunde, Sylvie and Alege with their two boys, Shaddak and El-Shadai, who are staying with friends in a village hidden from rebels. Alege walks two hours each way to our compound where he checks on the buildings, the animals and the crops; and of Paluku Sabuni, the senior staff member, and Unega, both of whom have responsible positions and therefore could be at risk. There are a few friends looking after the hospital but there are very few patients – not even those suffering from meningitis or cholera have the courage to go to the hospital. Even if they go, there are no medicines, as they were stolen (together with our radio) by rebels. Alege, trying to encourage me, tells me that my dog is safe (in hiding with another friend!). I want to sob, but this is not a time to express emotions – practical arrangements are more important: how to get cash to Nyankunde; what to do about the appalling water situation; how to cope with the cholera now there is no infrastructure; what contingency plans to make for the students.*

*War is cruel, and particularly for those already marginalised. They may not die of bullets (although they may), but death is waiting for them where normally health care would be available. Every pregnant woman becomes a woman at risk of dying (Alege tells me that a friend of mine has just died in childbirth – together with her child); every cholera case has a higher likelihood of dying than of surviving; malnourished children die with the first infection that comes along – or, for those under two years, there is a likelihood of their becoming educationally disabled (the child's brain should be developing up to this age). Chronically ill persons must live without treatment, and surgical emergencies can only be coped with in the absence of pain-killers or antibiotics. Cultivation and commerce cease, so food supplies are drastically affected; schooling stops; development programmes are arrested; and the poorest fall off the 'poverty cliff' and into the 'pit of despondency', from where, even after the war, it will be difficult to emerge again.*

*While I was training as a CMS mission partner (1970), I was not interested in the range of activities addressing the needs of the margin-alised or refugees. Rather I chose studies concerning the Christian approach to health and development, to wholeness and to justice issues. Now few of us have the choice as many mission partners will find themselves touching the lives of refugees or working in disaster areas. But what is the church in Europe doing about this whole area? I know that it is painful watching TV programmes of yet another tragedy with pictures of starving children, and feeling helpless in not knowing how to respond, nor knowing what has caused the crisis. But frequently we do not know what our own Government is up to. What, for example, does it mean to the Christian healing ministry in a developing country when an American rocket hits a town of innocent people, and when the British Government immediately applauds the action? At the site of impact there are probably hundreds dead and wounded and thou-sands homeless. Mission partners and other organisations' expatriate staff will be evacuated immediately – abandoning important pro-grammes. Health and development programmes are fractured, com-munications broken and the indispensable resources for ongoing work stuck in another country.*

*The pains and joys seen in my kaleidoscope blend into the overall canvas of God's purpose – but there are no scenes which show me what will happen next.*

### LL83: 20 March 1999

*But what was I doing in Uganda? The situation in the Democratic Republic of Congo (DRC) has remained unstable since we left in August of last year, and so CMS mission partners have not been able to return. However, work has continued. IPASC, with the diploma course in Nyankunde and the new university course in Bunia has 70 and 80 students respectively. Development activities such as the Safe*

*Motherhood Programme, the Water Protection project and the Institute's Farm, have seen renewed activities, although it is not easy for staff to move around. I am continually amazed by the achievements of my colleagues, but there comes a time when we need to meet and discuss progress, difficulties and plans for the future. This was the purpose of my trip to Uganda, where I met up with colleagues from DRC for ten days of meetings and working on accounts.*

*Philip Bingham, the accountant for the Anglican Province of Congo, joined us for a few days, and did an audit for us as well as advising us on several areas of financial management. Working with my colleagues has been refreshing and challenging.*

*The CMS mission partners outside the Congo, including myself, are feeling the effects of being 'refugees'. It is difficult to cope with the uncertainty of when we might be able to return, and to settle into other useful areas of work. However, it is very clear that this is not the time to return. In the past week there have been several cruel murders in the area in which the Institute is situated, and moving around is becoming increasingly difficult. We know that our presence in DRC would put our friends and colleagues at risk, and their concern for our safety would add to their already heavy workloads.*

*Although I regret not being able to return to DRC, it has been a good opportunity for me to work with a different set of colleagues in Côte d'Ivoire. The situation is very different, but there are many similarities with the early days of the programme in Congo. As yet, we have no buildings, but we have been able to borrow the nurses' home of the Methodist Hospital in Dabou, about an hour's drive from Abidjan. Like DRC, we are teaching in French, and have students from four West African countries (Togo, Gabon, Bénin and Côte d'Ivoire). I have needed to learn about the culture and have found that it is very different from DRC. For example, in Côte d'Ivoire I can never talk directly to a tribal chief, but must work through an intermediary (not because of language barriers, but because I am a woman and a commoner!). Animism and Islam are as strong, or stronger, than Christianity, while in Congo 95% of the population are Christians (at least by name). Côte d'Ivoire is relatively developed and the standard of living much higher than in Congo, and, indeed, than much of Africa. Yet adult education (and especially that of women) is low, and primary health care is still undeveloped. Major health problems include HIV/AIDS and heart disease, and social concerns focus on more typ-*

*ically 'developed country' problems such as paedophilia. Homosexuality is a common practice in the city, while almost unknown in Congo.*

### LL87: 1 February 2000

*We are used to wars and instability in the Democratic Republic of Congo (DRC) but who would have expected a coup d'état in Côte d'Ivoire? I had left the country just a few days before the Christmas Eve coup. At that time everything seemed calm, but there was a political restlessness as plans for forthcoming elections were tailored in favour of those in power. The military take-over seems to have been welcomed, especially as there is an assurance by the military leader that elections will go ahead this year as planned. My colleagues at IPASC (Côte d'Ivoire) assure me that they and their families remained safe (there were very few casualties of the coup) and that work was progressing well. Their only complaint was that they could not go to church on Christmas Eve! Compared with DRC it seems to have been a very 'lady-like' coup, but has also been very effective and very welcome! Before leaving Côte d'Ivoire we completed the second short course, and ensured that students could get back to their own countries (Bénin, Togo, Guinea (Conakry) and within Côte d'Ivoire) before Christmas.*

*My plan, on leaving Côte d'Ivoire, was to get to Nyankunde (DRC) for Christmas, but reports coming out of the country were not encouraging. The day I was dreading and longing for at the same time (23 December) arrived and I checked in at Entebbe (Kampala) airport for the flight to Bunia together with Jonathan, an American missionary friend. As we flew over Lake Albert and identified the lakeside town of Tchomia (the epicentre of cholera and well known to IPASC students!) Bunia seemed all too close! Within a few minutes we were on the ground.*

*There were soldiers everywhere – some extremely young. One little lad's (a Bunia boy soldier) army trousers were too long and, as he sat on a wall swinging his legs, I longed to put him in shorts and send him to school! As the door of the plane opened all the old airport staff appeared – the same rogues and friends were there. The immigration officer said 'Mama – why did you leave us for so long' and the friend who waves in the planes chastised me for not remembering to bring him some saccharine (he is diabetic). There were not many new faces except those of the soldiers. The IPASC staff were there in force together with Dave Jacobsson (MAF pilot) and his son Matthew – with whom I would be staying. I had to pay £60 for a visa for a month, but customs and immigration were otherwise harmless! We drove off – with me sighing with relief.*

*The IPASC (Bunia/University) staff had laid on a meal for us, but first I visited the students. I was amazed to find them in the Anglican Diocesan centre and church. Every room was adapted as a classroom or office and across the compound in the primary school was a mud hut for the 52 first-years. I was both impressed at their innovative measures and embarrassed that I had not been able to raise sufficient funds to provide them with classrooms on our own campus! It was just wonderful to see the students and the progress that the staff had made. This is the first time I had met any students of the university course, but now some are in their second year. Imagine being halfway through a university course and seeing your Director for the first time! There are now over 100 students.*

*At Nyankunde (25 muddy miles from Bunia: i.e. two hours drive) I stayed with Dave and Donna Jacobsson, who live about a mile from the IPASC campus. Each day I commuted via the airstrip on my four-wheeler motorbike. At IPASC I was overwhelmed – by the welcome from staff and students; by the wonderful progress of the building of the new refectory; of the improved agriculture; of the amazing herd of cows, the goats and chickens. The less welcome sight was the rebel camp on our grounds just below the students' hostel (replacing our 'model' cholera camp!). I missed my dog (who died a few months ago) and the house did not feel quite right without him. Some of the third-year students had cycled over 700 miles to get back to IPASC after having been stuck at home by the war! There are 20 new first-years which is the maximum number. This is encouraging after very few students in the third and second year.*

*I started to unpack what my colleagues had carefully put in boxes and hidden in the attic. There seemed to be no end to my possessions – especially clothes – and then I realised that I was seeing some things for the first time in years . . . many things had been hidden before the last war and I thought they were lost, so had invested in new clothes. Together with the things I left behind in August 1998 I had enough underwear to open a boutique (or rather, have a jumble sale)! I also found some of last year's Christmas presents for the staff – which was convenient since I had not brought any this year! I found a number of cheque books, mostly eaten by termites, my address book, my camera, my favourite books and loads of unanswered letters (apologies to all concerned). The house had been very carefully preserved, with all my personal belongings and family photos just as I left them. I now realise why the past year and a half have been so difficult for me. Everything that was special to me was in this house. Now some things had been spoilt or destroyed by damp or termites, but this did not matter. I could just throw these things away, but at least I was in control. In the cupboard were the remains of a jar of home-made marmalade which almost exploded when I opened the lid!*

*Christmas at Nyankunde was simple and lovely, and I enjoyed just being among friends and being in my own home during the daytime. But, while Christmas at Nyankunde was special, more treats were to come.*

*On 30 December, together with colleagues, I left Nyankunde for Boga. We travelled along the rough roads, sometimes hardly visible between the overgrown grasses and the deep mud. We wove our way through the hills – as beautiful as ever – stopping at health centres to greet friends and to leave some medical supplies. We got badly stuck in the mud a couple of times (nothing new!) and were pushed and dug out by villagers happy to earn a few pence. Halfway along the five-hour (60-mile) drive, we decided not to make any more social visits – there were just too many people to greet and we were getting late for the wedding of Archbishop Njojo's son Kahwa, and Nene, an IPASC University student. Eventually we arrived at Boga an hour or so after the beginning of the wedding. We sat through another three hours, but it was a beautiful service. Nen looked lovely – but so sad (as is the custom!). Kahwa had grown from a little boy to a young man in two years! The packed cathedral was decorated with banana trees and flowers. It was one of the best weddings I have ever attended. It was led by Bishop Isingoma – who is presently a refugee from his diocese of Katanga where he had been severely tortured. It was good to see so many special friends at the same time, but difficult to talk to everyone at once, and to take everything in. The feast following the wedding was also special. I looked anxiously among the crowds for Neema and Rehema (our two girls – now sixteen years old). Neema found me first. She was as tall as me, and looked very grown up. Rehema is taller than me, as quiet as Neema is talkative, and looks very attractive. Seeing them after so long was both painful and special!*

*Later I visited the Archbishop's elderly father, and then made my way up to Nyakabale, to the Kabarole home. Nyangoma had not come to the wedding, knowing that it would be too long for her. She looked reasonably well but not as well as I had expected. She was managing her peritoneal dialysis well. That evening she developed peritonitis, so much of the rest of my time at Boga was spent nursing her at home.*

*We passed into the new Millennium in silence and concern – more aware of Nyangoma than the time but within three days she was beginning to improve. On New Year's Day (during the five-hour service at the cathedral!) we were informed of the sudden and unexpected death of the Bishop of Kinshasa, Bishop Mavatikwa. This is a tragic loss of a faithful and hard-working Bishop, friend, husband and father.*

*I had to return to Nyankunde on 3 January, ready to begin teaching. On the way back we stopped at Bukaringi to drop off some medical supplies. I then went down to the Archdeacon's house. The family did not know I was in the area, but their response to my 'hodi' was somewhat tumultuous. The whole family was there: seven children, two wives and five grandchildren. They have always been special friends of mine. Simon (named after Bishop Simon Barrington-Ward), now eight years old, shadowed me, telling me all about his progress at school. Neema, now eighteen, asked if she could come to study at IPASC next year. I had meant to stay for ten minutes, but an hour later, and with several chickens in hand, we left. There were many other friends to see, including the lad who used to help me in my house at Boga. He is now a young widower with three children. All along the road to Nyankunde there were shouts and waving. We then stopped at Longba '. . . just for two minutes'. Anyasi, the midwife, said that we had to stay for at least 'three minutes' since lunch was already on the table. Another hour later we left – full of good food and love, and with chicken and a sack of sweet potatoes adding to our luggage. Eventually we arrived at Nyankunde. What a journey – just packed with love all the way along the tortuous track through the beautiful hills of Ituri.*

*Days at Nyankunde assumed a routine. Up between 5.30 and 6am; student and staff prayers at 7.30am and teaching from 8am until midday and from 1.30pm to 4.30pm. There were also administrative jobs, and the hospital staff wanted help with some problems. Commuting from my hill-top missionary flat on my sometimes unreliable four-wheeler was becoming a frustration, so I moved down to my own house on the IPASC compound. It was wonderful!*

*There were at least two weddings each weekend. One was that of*

*Jean Bachumas and Emeline, Burundian students and refugees who have just completed studies at IPASC. Sadly, Jean and Emeline's ethnic background puts them at risk in Eastern Congo and even more so in Burundi. But today, they put aside their anxieties. The wedding was beautiful. The local Christians had rewarded them for their warmth and collaboration by providing a dress for Emeline and a suit for Jean. The church put on a wonderful reception for 500 people. For a day, this humble couple were in the limelight, and we all enjoyed seeing them look so radiantly happy – no customary unhappiness for Emeline! The tragedy is that probably they will have to leave us within the next few weeks, since Immigration are being difficult about their being here, and are charging £100 each, every three months, for visas. They have no money and we cannot afford to pay for them any longer as we have no scholarship money.*

*All too soon, it was time for me to leave Congo. Sabuni was coming with me to Kampala, to register for his PhD at Makerere University. We drove from Bunia to the mining area 20 miles away where we were to meet another vehicle coming from another direction. We were early so looked round the very dilapidated mines. Clearly the machinery was once very sophisticated. There had been deterioration until the present war, but now everything was wrecked. Local villages were using artesian methods of sifting earth, looking for a few crumbs of gold. Eventually the other vehicle arrived and we joined the travellers (and Jonathan and his daughter, with whom I travelled into the Congo).*

*The road was horrific. The large transporters had carved into the soft mud and now there were sculptured walls reaching halfway up the windows of our land cruiser. We were forced into the ruts, and, as we tried to negotiate our way along, we were thrown from one side to the other. Sabuni and I were sharing a seat, so I could not wear a seat belt. I hit my head repeatedly on the window. Many times we had to get out into the deep mud to check the depth of an area full of water. We managed to cover fifteen miles in two hours!*

*Eventually we reached Fataki, and the end of the worst of the quagmire. We stopped to buy 'barbecued' chicken (roasted in charcoal in the middle of the market). I recognised the Fataki Hospital vehicle, but as I walked towards it to greet old friends, I discovered it was full of soldiers (Ugandans). I withdrew quickly. Meanwhile, Jonathan was in a heated discussion with some men (no women were around). Sabuni and I moved away, not wanting to get caught in an argument.*

*Apparently the men had told Jonathan to find his 'Red Cross friends' and tell them not to come near the town, because 'if they do they will be cut up into small pieces and thrown to the dogs!' This then was the beginning of the tribal war zone (a war that is now twelve months old). This group was very angry because they said the Red Cross had brought supplies for the opposing tribe and not for them (this was not true). We drove on carefully. Fortunately, the road was much better. Then we came to burnt houses . . . hundreds of them; fields were ruined; three were destroyed. There was sheer devastation everywhere. Few people could have survived the slaughter. We had heard that over 50,000 had been killed and over twice that number had fled (many we had seen in Bunia) and were now homeless. We met a band of about 30 young men (the opposite tribe to those met in Fataki). The people in this tribe are mostly illiterate, and usually marginalised. They all carried bows and poisoned arrows, and, as they heard the vehicle, they drew up their bows and aimed at us. Jonathan opened his window quickly and spoke gently in Swahili to the frightened group, so convincing them that we were friends. We all followed, and shared our greetings. The men thanked us for driving through and encouraging them. A little later we came across some soldiers and gave one a lift. They were Ugandans who had come about a week previously to calm the war, and were cutting trees and grass, to open up the road and to reduce the risk of aggressors hiding in the scrub. A few kilometres further on we came to a stream. On the other side (in another tribal territory), life was very normal. What an amazing contrast!*

*At 4pm we reached the border. There was no one else crossing so we hoped to get through quickly. After an hour, and many frustrating conversations, when the immigration team tried to find fault with each passport and looked for ways to fine us, we made it clear that we knew that their Bunia chiefs were in prison for corruption . . . We were through five minutes later! Ten minutes later we were at the Paidha (Ugandan post). There we were welcomed by a bright, smart immigration officer, and had completed formalities in less than five minutes! We drove into town for a meal (beans and plantain) and then 20 miles to an Anglican mission where we found beds (four of us, men and women, in the same room!). We were shattered and full of emotions of what we had seen . . . all of us slept well.*

*In Kampala I was able to spend some time at the Provincial Synod (the fact that the Anglican Church of Congo had to have its Synod in*

*Uganda reminds us of the major difficulties of insecurity and poor communications in Congo). This was another special time of meeting with old friends, as well as seeing friends from Boga Diocese, with whom I had spent the past few weeks. Nyangoma was there, completely healed and with far more energy than I could muster!*

*Now I am teaching at the Liverpool School of Tropical Medicine for a month (what a contrast!) . . . and at the end of March will be returning to Côte d'Ivoire for the next IPASC course there. During my time in England, a group of friends from St Mary's, Upton (our parish church), with representation from CMS, will be helping me work through some of the management issues posed by my rather complex peripatetic lifestyle, with responsibilities in Côte d'Ivoire, DR Congo and Liverpool. I really appreciate this initiative and the concern of these friends. Pray that under new management, an efficient and realistic division of time and effort will develop.*

## LL88: 20 April 2000

*Greetings from Abidjan, Côte d'Ivoire! Because of my 'no fixed abode' status I have left my home address at the top of this letter – but Abidjan is very different from the Wirral. It is hot and steamy, the markets are noisy and dirty, and the enormous volume of traffic causes traffic jams even late at night. But Abidjan is one of the most efficient cities of West Africa, with a good communications system, and somewhat Parisian lifestyle (in some quarters). It has a large port and a significant tourist trade, attracting foreigners to its golden, palm-lined beaches. I will be here for a month, firstly working on the development of our programme in Abidjan and then teaching for the first two weeks of our third three-month course in Dabou. We have nearly 30 students coming, with more booking for the next course (which is not even planned!). They include those from Congo (Kinshasa), Central African Republic, Bénin, Togo, Guinea (Conakry) and Côte d'Ivoire, and from diverse disciplines, from doctors to pastors and a commercial trader – though most are health professionals.*

*Bishop David Urquhart lays the foundation stone for IPASC in Aru, 2003*

# CHAPTER 7

# Peace and Progress

The consequences of conflict brought an end to the work of IPASC in Côte d'Ivoire, though the IPASC resources were left to be used by IPASC partners. In DRC, it opened up new challenges and opportunities to respond to needs within the community and with different churches in a time of relative peace. Leadership within the team developed and new collaborative relationships were formed.

Looking ahead, I felt it right to step down as Executive Director of IPASC so that I had time to accompany the person who would take my place. I had not anticipated that I was being called into ordained ministry at that time, nor what God was doing in the area of reconciliation through the church.

---

*Should include the Boga reconciliation.*
*A resurrection community in Aru, Bunia, Boga, and Upton – a different triangulation (so includes reconciliation, fistulae, rape, safe motherhood and other operational programmes).*

*Pat's ordination, Chester Cathedral, July 2004. Bishop David Urquhart, Pat, sister Nikki, Canon Rob Shimwell*

*Pat with Amoti Kabarole, Aru, 2007*

*Pat and Philippa Skinner in Aru with Bishop Henri Isingoma Kahwa, then Bishop of Boga, and his diocesan staff, 2008: Pat's last visit to DRC*

*A visit to some dear friends, the Catholic Sisters of Aru, 2008*

# CHAPTER 8

# A Pilgrimage

Selection for ordination in both the Dioceses of Boga and Chester, and training in the UK and Kenya were the beginning of a new journey. They were not part of my plans for handing over the leadership of IPASC. Unexpectedly God's plans took me into parish and Diocesan life in the Dioceses of Chester (UK), and Boga and Aru (DRC), which led the Bishop of Chester to propose that I work on creating a link between Chester, Boga and Aru, which gained the support of the other Bishops (and broad support within the parishes of the three dioceses). However, an even more unexpected change was that, not too far into my new vocation, I was diagnosed with cancer, for which treatment could only be prophylactic. The sense of peace equipped me in an exciting way for the walk ahead of me. Sharing some of those experiences can only be expressed in terms of a pilgrimage.

## The Glade: A Relational Walk

The miracle of healing, living a normal life within view and changing parameters or horizons. I'm grateful for prayer but I don't want to be dragged back through the glade because the light is in front of me. A much more organised life – lists written, things done, timing right, things put away.

SET YOUR HOPE ON THE GRACE THAT IS COMING
TO YOU AT THE REVELATION OF JESUS CHRIST
I PETER 1.13.

## Dying and Resurrection

*Written by Pat at the end of March 2009*

In late August 2007, I was four days away from international travel. Slight abdominal discomfort took me to the GP simply to confirm that I was not 'cooking' something serious. 'You may find that you can't travel', said the very bright and sympathetic GP, who offered to talk more once she had finished the evening surgery. After the initial shock I recognised that I, who was usually fit and full of energy, was being told that I probably had a terminal illness.

Eighteen months further on, with failed surgery and treatment behind me, I am on a pilgrimage which has given me a new and exciting relationship with God. It has taken me, and continues to take me, through a Glade in which peace reigns and the process of dying and resurrection have become a way of life which I want to share with those who are frightened of talking about dying.

Before going any further, however, it is important that we identify areas in our lives where we cannot make comparisons, and where differences in our backgrounds mean that we cannot expect similarities which will help us to accept terminal or serious illness in the same way. Circumstances that may make us very different and thus incomparable include:

- Family: Having/not having a living spouse or dependants.
- Life-experiences: Having lived through dangers, isolation and other lifestyle risks.
- Health: Living in situations in which health care is not given the highest priority.
- Faith: The importance we give to our faith-lives will make a difference to our view of death. ·

Being generally relaxed, positive and at peace (how we approach life) will have an effect on how we approach dying.

### *Here are a few principles and issues that we need to discuss*

### 1. To live is Christ, to die is gain (Philippians 1.21–23)
Christ was the source and secret of Paul's continual joy (even in prison), for Paul's life found all its meaning in Christ. He specifies that the gain brought by death is 'being with Christ' – his ultimate concern and most precious possession, both now and always, is Christ and his relationship with him (Philippians 1.23). So why is it so difficult for us to talk about or to confront death? For each of us the answer will be different.

### 2. Changing horizons
For the dying person, as well as for the carer, horizons are changing.

For the carer, horizons (the approaching death event – if it can be anticipated) may be getting closer too quickly because of the fear of loss and the longing to hold on to the hope of healing (and continuing bodily presence).

For the sick loved one, horizons may be being pushed away through prayer and caring (often by the close carer), while the sick person may prefer to draw the horizons towards him/herself – an indication of a readiness to meet God.

## 3. Prayer

The sick person and the carer's felt need of prayer (for the dying person) may differ considerably. Someone on a pilgrimage with a special and growing relationship with God may be praying that his/her response to the beckoning Light at the end of the Glade, will give a tangible peace that will encourage others. The carer may want complete healing for the loved one, suggesting that they want to see the loved one pulled back through the Glade to resume a new, completely restored life. But what does God want to give? My walk has been so special, as has the peace that goes with it. I would not want to be 'pulled back' through the Glade, but rather to walk on into the beckoning Light.

For me the Christian life is a pilgrimage during which we confront the challenges and opportunities of this world (Revelation 3.10). Dying is a part of that pilgrimage where I see myself walking through a Glade, where the sunshine/Light beckons me on, but is clouded by mist, which is the mystery of passing from the Glade through to the Resurrection.

*Pat died on Sunday, 26 April 2009, just four weeks after writing this chapter.*

# CHAPTER 9

# Final Days

Pat wrote: 'Difficult to write at this stage.'

## The Sisters of Jesus Way* tell of Pat's last days

Pat had made plans for her dying. She hoped she would be with the Sisters and cared for by her own GP, for whom she had a deep regard. Despite increasing pain, which was becoming more and more difficult to control, she felt that she would probably live until June 2009, still three months away. Valuing her independence, she was living alone in her flat. Sister Marie rang her morning and evening. The telephone conversations invariably turned to sharing her journey with God. Always wanting to learn more, she applied this to the serious business of dying. She faced her homecoming to God calmly and with anticipation, although she shrank – as we all do – from the suffering.

Early in April she visited us and gave Communion to a 98-year-old lady, the grandmother of Lynda, one of the Sisters. Afterwards, she came straight on to the community motherhouse to encourage and comfort in a tragic situation they were experiencing. It was costly, walking was difficult, and increasingly strong drugs were only barely controlling the pain. Self-giving to the last, these were probably her last pastoral visits.

A few days later (14 April) she rang about 9.30pm obviously distressed and asking for help. Sisters Sylvia and Marie were soon

---

\* A community of Sisters living near Upton in Wirral who wonderfully supported Pat throughout her illness.

at her flat. Martin, an associate vicar at St Mary's, was already there. There was no alternative but to hastily pack some things and call for an ambulance. She was taken to Arrowe Park Hospital, Wirral. In the early hours of the morning she was given a bed in a surgical assessment unit.

The next day she was transferred to a busy surgical ward. It was decided that there would be no surgical intervention. It was obvious that her condition was steadily worsening. Her bleak comment one day was, 'What a mess I am in.' Yet she still managed to give pastoral care and support to other patients. More than a few were grateful for her presence on the ward. To the relief of friends, she was transferred to St John's Hospice, Wirral, on Tuesday 21 April.

No one, including Pat herself, expected that this was to be her last week of life. Her beautiful single room looked out on the courtyard. Perhaps Bishop Keith Sinclair described it best when he said that he could feel Jesus in the room. Most of the unpleasant symptoms had been quickly brought under control under expert care. Pat's thoughts turned to the book she was hoping to complete. On Thursday 23 April she asked for her laptop to be brought in. By evening, however, her condition had suddenly and unexpectedly deteriorated. She was fully aware but could only manage to speak the odd word.

She deteriorated further through the night. On Friday morning the hospice contacted her relatives and close friends. From that moment Pat was never left, by day or night. The love of God surrounded her. After a long drive from the south of England, Pat's brother, Gordon, arrived late on Friday evening. He too, apart from a few necessary hours of sleep, never left her side. Her sister, Nikki, started the journey from Australia, but sadly arrived after Pat had died.

Early on Saturday morning those who were accompanying Pat on this final part of her pilgrimage gathered together around her bed. The hospice nurse who had special responsibility for Pat joined them. A short service was held including Bible readings, prayers, anointing with oil and the triumphant Easter acclamation, 'Christ is risen'. Although her ability to communicate had almost gone, from the few words that could be understood, we knew she was fully aware of all that was happening.

At 10.45pm there was a knock on the door. It was Remy and Annette Toko who had been her dear friends and colleagues in DR Congo. They had made the journey from Hull to say goodbye to Pat, leaving their three children asleep at home.

On Sunday morning (26th) the Bishop of Chester, Peter Forster, arrived. As his hands folded around Pat's hands, he echoed the voices of many when with feeling he said not once but several times, 'Dear Pat'. The ancient prayers of the church from the old prayer book were read as Pat slowly slipped away from us. Sister Lynda sang quietly, 'The Lord bless you, the Lord keep you, the Lord make his face to shine upon you and be gracious to you. The Lord be radiant with joy because of you, the Lord lift up his countenance upon you and give you peace.' The Lord was merciful, and several hours later her sufferings were over; He had taken her home.

*Detective Sergeant Eleanor Essay demonstrates handcuffing at a talk about her job to Pat and other members of the Cancer Support Group meeting at the Sisters of Jesus Way, West Kirby, Wirral, 2008*

## Thanksgiving Service,
## St Mary's Church, Upton, Wirral, 5 May 2009

*Revd Graeme Skinner takes a phone call from Elias Assia in Aru. Tim Dakin*
*(then General Secretary, CMS) looks on from the lectern where he was speaking.*

*Revd Graeme Skinner and Bishop Keith Sinclair welcoming everyone in*
*English and Swahili*

# Celebration of Pat's life and dedication of the Nickson Room at Liverpool School of Tropical Medicine, 30 January 2010

*Pat's brother, Gordon (pictured) and other family members attended this great occasion*

# 'Inspired': A Postscript

## Philippa Skinner

I knew Pat for just under three years. I have learned that you can't measure the significance of a friendship by its length alone, however, as Pat taught me so much in that short time.

I was privileged to travel to DR Congo with her twice, once in April 2007 and again in August 2008. On the first occasion my husband Graeme was also with us. In those two weeks we lapped up all Pat could teach us and tell us about her years in Congo. She opened our eyes to so much by generously sharing her experiences and patiently answering our endless questions. We were like two small children sitting at their elder's knee, listening hard and drinking it all in! I think Pat was thrilled to share her life in this way too, and in those weeks a deep friendship bond was established. On one occasion we visited the IPASC campus at Bunia, but found we were too late for the students – I think they were on their Easter break – so we were unable to greet them. Pat was sorry to miss them and wrote a quick message on the blackboard as evening darkness fell, 'We will come back again to see you.'

Sadly, not long after this trip, Pat's illness was diagnosed, and there were months of great physical hardship for her as she battled courageously with the treatment and the disease.

However, Pat was determined she would go back to Congo to see her many friends there at least once again, and she invited me to go with her in August 2008. My role on that occasion was very much 'bag carrier'. At least that was the way I saw it, but not surprisingly to those who knew her, I found Pat to be determined to do as much for herself as she possibly could and to look after me into the bargain! That was an amazing journey in so many ways and on so many levels.

We were constantly on the move, from leaving home at 3am on Monday morning until Thursday afternoon. The first leg was Manchester to Uganda, where we arrived at midnight on Monday to discover that Pat's bag was lost. Thereafter we travelled from Arua to Aru, to Boga, to Bukaringi, back to Boga, to Nyankunde and on to Bunia. Finally we returned to Aru where we became a little more sedentary on and around the IPASC campus for the remaining days of the trip. How Pat found the energy for such travels I will never know – she was amazing.

In a visit which was so deeply moving, perhaps one of the most moving moments came when we returned to IPASC at Bunia. The students swarmed out en masse, overjoyed to welcome Pat. 'You said you would come back to see us. We knew you would keep your word!' That blackboard message had been treasured and remembered. We were so grateful that Pat had indeed been able to go back again to see them and honour that hastily written message.

Pat longed to go again in the early months of 2009, but sadly it became clear that would not be possible. However, she had, against the odds, been able to return in 2008, and say and do what she needed and wanted to do, and that was a great joy and comfort to her Congolese friends.

For me, to be able to accompany her on that trip was a great privilege and a most memorable and inspirational part of my life. At this point I don't know if I will ever be able to return again to DR Congo, but what I learned through Pat and her many friends there taught me so much which I hope I will never forget, and which I trust will continue to inspire me in the years ahead.

# Timeline of Pat's Life

| Year | Events |
|------|--------|
| 1944 | Birth |
| 1955 | Royal Masonic School, Rickmansworth |
| 1962 | Nurse/midwife training |
| 1965 | Mobutu becomes President of Zaïre |
| 1969 | Northern Territory, Australia, work experience |
| 1970 | Crowther Hall, Birmingham, CMS training |
| 1971 | Afghanistan, Yakaolang valley |
| 1971 | Belgian Congo renamed Zaïre |
| 1975 | Bangladesh, Bollobhpur |
| 1980 | Zaïre, feasibility study group |
| 1981 | Jamaica, study trip |
| 1982 | Zaïre, Boga |
| 1983 | Zaïre, Bukavu |
| 1983 | Zaïre, N Kivu, evaluation |
| 1984 | Zaïre, Aru, confirmation safari |
| 1985 | Zaïre Government inspection |
| 1986 | Liverpool, PhD, 'Local Definition of Health' |
| 1989 | Geneva, Christian Medical Commission |
| 1990 | Bénin, CMC workshop |
| 1991 | Geneva, World Health Assembly |
| 1991 | Nigeria, conference |
| 1991 | Central African Republic |
| 1991 | Tchad |
| 1991 | Tanzania |
| 1991 | Zaïre, back to Boga |
| 1991 | Liverpool School of Tropical Medicine, Senior Lecturer |

| Year | Events |
|------|--------|
| 1992 | Birth of Pan-African Institute of Community Health (IPASC) |
| 1992 | Njojo appointed first Archbishop of Zaïre |
| 1993 | Conflict in Boga |
| 1994 | Pat houses 20 refugees from Rwanda |
| 1996 | Pat in Goma – a million refugees |
| 1996 | Nyankunde pillaged and burnt in tribal attack |
| 1996 | Shooting incident in hangar |
| 1996 | IPASC evacuates foreign staff and students |
| 1997 | Mobutu into exile, Laurent Kabila becomes President |
| 1997 | Zaïre name changed to Democratic Republic of Congo |
| 1997 | Return to Congo |
| 1998 | Pat has malaria and typhus |
| 1998 | Pat evacuated from Congo |
| 1998 | Pat a refugee in Uganda |
| 1998 | IPASC expands to Cote d'Ivoire |
| 1999 | Sabuni awarded scholarship for PhD |
| 1999 | First proposals for a supporting Trust in UK |
| 2000 | Nyankunde room opened at LSTM |
| 2000 | Pat returns to Nyankunde |
| 2000 | Friends of IPASC formed |
| 2000 | Coup d'état in Côte d'Ivoire |
| 2001 | IPASC Board of Governors formed with Pat as Dean |
| 2002 | Evacuation of IPASC from Nyankunde |
| 2003 | Evacuation of IPASC from Bunia |
| 2004 | Pat ordained Deacon in Chester Cathedral |
| 2005 | Pat ordained Priest in Aru |
| 2005 | Pat awarded OBE in New Year's Honours List |
| 2007 | Diagnosis of terminal cancer |
| 2008 | Elias becomes Executive Director of IPASC |
| 2009 | Died on 26 April in St John's Hospice, Wirral |

# Notes

1 32 years later, Shondha and Tara are still an important part of my life, and now have their own stories to tell.
2 Infusion in water gives low psychoactive effects. This is raised by adding milk or other fats or oils.
3 Keloyi Kabarole, whose 'mpako' (pet-name) is Amoti. There are twelve mpakos in Hema tradition, with no gender difference. The mpako is given to a child at birth, and is used among friends and family, implying both affection and respect.
4 Each clergyman had up to 26 churches in his parish.
5 'Obusinge' is a word from the Kihema language (the majority language of Boga), while Kisembo, whose family lived in Boga, was from the Ngity tribe.
6 The tribal Chief in charge of the Collectivity of Boga, which had a population of 10,000.
7 The values were established by the community leaders.
8 A Collectivity, headed by a Chief, is the lowest level of administrative, financial and legislative authority.
9 Some children had to walk up to seven miles to school.
10 Later to become the Region of South Kivu.
11 Later to become the Region of North Kivu.
12 Tuberculosis, polio, diphtheria, tetanus, whooping cough and measles.
13 The Nursing School.
14 The Anglican Church of Zaïre, now the Province of the Anglican Church of Congo.
15 *Healing and Wholeness: The Churches' Role in Health.* The report of a study by the Christian Medical Commission of the World Council of Churches, Geneva, 1990, p1.

16 *'The Baby Killer': An Investigation into the Promotion and Sale of Powdered Baby Milks in the Third World* by Mike Muller. March 1974. Published and printed by War on Want, 467 Caledonian Road, London N7 9BE.

17 Known as the Belgian Congo until independence in 1960, and then The Congo. Mobutu changed the name to Zaïre in 1971, while also creating a new national identity in details such as dress code and 'authentic' personal names. His fall from power in 1997 saw a reversal to the use of Congo (the name Kongo originally being that of the mighty River Zaïre, 'the river that swallows all rivers') which became the Democratic Republic of the Congo (confusion with the neighbouring Republic of Congo needing to be avoided). http://en.wikipedia.org/wiki/Zaïre.

18 http://www.nyankunde.org/english05.htm.

19 The word for peace in Kihema, the local language, was 'obusinge' – which means 'that which encapsulated the whole of life'.

20 The Collectivity is the smallest unit of civil society. Headed by a tribal Chief, usually through inherited leadership, though popular agreement may also be used when the next-in-line does not seem to be the most appropriate leader.

21 Apolo was the first Anglican missionary in Congo, sent from the church in Uganda.

22 A clan is a unit of a group of families within the same tribe.

23 The American group to which our work in Afghanistan was affiliated.

24 Later, Elise also became an IPASC staff member.

25 To become Executive Director in 2008.

26 I think these are 'hired' by the church (if it is the Mekena Yesus programme of the Western Synod). Hiring through the church, as in the Ethiopian experience, is much more exciting and potentially sustainable because the church is known not to have money, whereas it is assumed that health programmes have lots of money!

27 The Kabarole household was known as a safe and welcoming place for all tribes, but anyone taking advantage of the hospitality was expected to be ready to share with anyone else in the home.

I had been away from Boga for four years, sometimes in England, often in Geneva, but for most of the time waltzing around Africa like a VIP, receiving amazing amounts of attention, when it was really all about listening to communities, like those with whom I had shared today, and feeling their pain and poverty. We were in for another storm and it felt as though the windows of my room would break with its force. It felt as though the windows of my heart would break too. Had I been a traitor to these people I loved so much, or could our mutual love, which now stretched across continents and oceans, enable us to take an important message to the world?

*Pat Nickson, July 1991*